Critical Guides to French Texts

138   Vailland: Un Jeune Homme seul *and* 325 000 francs

Critical Guides to French Texts

EDITED BY ROGER LITTLE, †WOLFGANG VAN EMDEN, DAVID WILLIAMS

VAILLAND

Un Jeune Homme seul
and
325 000 francs

David Nott

Emeritus Professor of French Language Studies
Lancaster University

London
Grant & Cutler Ltd 2005

© Grant & Cutler Ltd 2005

ISBN 0 7293 0448 5

DEPÓSITO LEGAL: V. 2.012 - 2005

Printed in Spain by
Artes Gráficas Soler, S.L., Valencia
for
GRANT & CUTLER LTD
55–57 GREAT MARLBOROUGH STREET, LONDON W1F 7AY

Contents

Prefatory note

References given in parentheses (italicised number followed by page reference) are to numbered items in the Select Bibliography.

Unless otherwise identified, page references in chapter 3 are to Roger Vailland, *Un Jeune Homme seul*, Paris, Grasset, Les Cahiers Rouges, 1992 (200pp), and in chapter 4 to Roger Vailland, *325 000 francs*, Paris, Livre de Poche, 1993 (244pp).

I am indebted to Professor Roger Little for his constructive editorial comments and advice; any shortcomings in what follows are, of course, attributable to me alone.

I am grateful to the British Academy for the award of a Small Research Grant which enabled me to spend several days consulting the Vailland archive in Bourg en Bresse.

Last but not least, je tiens à exprimer ma vive reconnaissance à Françoise Ferrand, chargée du fonds Vailland, et à Joëlle Rodet, bibliothécaire, de la Médiathèque Elisabeth et Roger Vailland, Bourg en Bresse, pour leur accueil toujours amical et leur aide attentionnée et efficace.

Lancaster   *DON*

Introduction

Un Jeune Homme seul (1951) and *325 000 francs* (1955) were written during the period of Vailland's close association with, and membership of, the Parti communiste français (PCF). Together with *Beau Masque* (1954), they stand as an example, relatively rare in literature, of a series of novels, written to serve overt political ends, which possess an intensity and unity of personal vision, a coherence of characterisation and overall structure, and an unfailing clarity and directness of style. Half a century after their publication, they conjure up vividly for the reader certain defining features of the society in which they are set.

These novels were written by an author who, in 1950, had made the bold statement that 'Il faut avoir l'audace de dire qu'il n'y a pas de culture en dehors du peuple' (*28*, p.194), and had declared, later the same year, in a letter to Pierre Courtade: 'Dans les circonstances actuelles, il n'est plus possible, pour moi, comme pour toi, d'écrire autrement que dans une perspective totalement communiste' (*28*, p.271). The sincerity, even naivety, of Vailland's commitment as a writer during these years is shown in an exchange with a factory worker in 1953: 'Un ouvrier: On parle de collaboration écrivain-ouvrier. Est-elle possible? / Vailland: Mais oui. Dites-nous ce que vous aimez lire, qui vous aimez lire. On essaiera de vous faire une littérature claire et utile, de vous montrer les choses comme elles sont pour vous faire comprendre comme elles devraient être' (quoted in *39*, p.381). Vailland himself recalled in 1964 that: 'quand j'écrivais *325 000 francs*, un militant d'Oyonnax me présenta dans une maison ouvrière: Roger Vailland, un écrivain au service du peuple, et j'en fus réellement ému' (*28*, p.753).

Such statements suggest that more was at stake for Vailland than a philosophical or ideological choice. From 1942, when he entered the Resistance, Vailland's conception of himself and his stake in the world became dependent on a threefold conjunction: seeing History as a progressive process, investing certain groups and individuals with the heroic capacity to be the midwives of History, and anchoring himself in History through association with these groups and individuals. By the time he came to write *Un Jeune Homme seul*, the triple link seemed to have been forged: association with the PCF's struggle gave him an external anchorage and a personal sense of dignity, whatever unresolved conflicts remained within him. The vulnerability of Vailland's position was that he conceived his place in History in terms of fusion and identification, rather than as a dynamic relation between two irreducibly distinct entities (self and not-self), a relation which, if it is to thrive, has constantly to be put in question. By seeking to replace the solitude of being an individual in the world by the intensity of fusion with an entity as all-embracing as History, he ran the risk that, sooner or later, he would become History's orphan, as was the case after 1956.

1. Vailland in his life and times

The family environment in which Roger-François Vailland (1907–65) grew up was middle-class, conservative and Catholic, and did its best to protect him from the outside world of workers, strikes, war and revolution, and their aftermath. The vital early bond with his mother, Anna, was abruptly perturbed when, on doctor's orders to protect her health, he was weaned at four months (*34*, p.20). Starting school was an ordeal, and he was withdrawn until the following year. For four years Vailland's father was away serving in the territorial infantry at Dunkerque, leaving his son all too victorious on the home front: 'Il était l'homme, le maître. Mémé-Gâteau était à ses genoux, et il est devenu amoureux de sa mère' (Geneviève Vailland, *34*, p.33). The end of the Great War brought Georges home, and ended Vailland's four-year reign. However, in the spring of 1919, when he fell ill with influenza, his parents' care and concern enabled him to set aside his hostility towards his father. Beginning in 1920–21, he formed, with three classmates at the Reims *lycée* (Lecomte, Daumal and Meyrat), a close-knit anti-conformist group, the 'phrères simplis-tes': his first experience of acceptance in a group outside his own family. Roger Gilbert-Lecomte, the undisputed leader of this group, was to have a profound and lasting influence on Vailland, who wrote in 1956: 'Il faut dire que j'ai aimé Roger Gilbert-Lecomte, je crois d'amour' (*28*, p.498; see also *34*, pp.65–70, and Lecomte's letter of 1923 to Vailland, *42*, pp.29–34). Lecomte introduced Vailland to the poetry and prose of Rimbaud (1854–91), whose influence is seen in the poems that Vailland wrote during this period, in his intention to write a *thèse de diplôme* on Rimbaud (see *29*, p.121), in Eugène-Marie's recourse to passages from Rimbaud at moments of tension and crisis in *Un Jeune Homme seul*, and in many other occasions when Vailland writes about French society as if from a non-European standpoint.

In 1925, Vailland entered the *lycée* Louis-le-Grand in Paris to prepare for the Ecole Normale Supérieure. Among his fellow pupils was Robert Brasillach (executed in 1945 for his enthusiastic collaboration during the Occupation), with whom he shared a lifelong passion for the tragedies of Corneille (1606–84) — in particular for *Le Cid* (1636) and its hero Don Rodrigue, whose name and deeds are invoked in several of Vailland's novels, including *325 000 francs*. In Vailland's words: 'La clef du *Jeune Homme seul* c'est la référence à Corneille comme préférence littéraire d'Eugène-Marie Favart' (*28*, p.443). After a serious bout of scarlet fever in the spring of 1927, he left the ENS and registered for a *licence* at the Sorbonne. In Paris, the 'phrères simplistes' reformed, discovered Surrealism, and planned their own review, *Le Grand Jeu*; the first issue appeared in 1928. In the same year, he obtained his *licence de philosophie* and began writing articles, mainly on society trivia, for the daily *Paris-Midi*. An article in September, calling the Paris police chief, Chiappe, 'l'épurateur de notre capitale', led to his exclusion from the Surrealist movement, at a meeting in March 1929 chaired by André Breton and attended by Aragon. The purpose of this exclusion, ostensibly pronounced for having shown approval of the Establishment, was to discredit, even to break up, the *Grand Jeu* group. The manoeuvre succeeded: Lecomte wrote to Daumal ruling out individual initiatives by group members, 'de peur des conneries genre Vailland qui ruinent notre montante renommée. Donc nous deux collaborons et nous seulement jusqu'à nouvel ordre' (*42*, p.194). This double exclusion, and the resultant sense of betrayal, were traumatic for Vailland: he turned to drug-taking, and this contributed to the ending of a three-year relationship with Marianne Lams ('Mimouchka'), five years his senior. In 1930, an infection in his right arm paralysed his hand; from hospital, he wrote to his mother that 'il y a quelque chose qu'on appelle la jeunesse et qui est fini pour moi' (*29*, p.191). His unstable lifestyle throughout the 1930s, both before and after his meeting and marriage in 1935–36 with Andrée Blavette, a nightclub singer, did nothing to free him from the grip of two long-established cyclical processes: mounting anxiety and depression from the onset of autumn to the year's end, and alternation between periods of depression and spells of elation.

After the fall of France in June 1940, Vailland followed the staff of *Paris-Soir*, to Marseille, then to Lyon. Like many French people in 1940–41, Vailland envisaged collaboration (*34*, p.253); from December 1941 to October 1942 he contributed articles to the *pétainiste* weekly *Présent*. Under the influence of an intellectual milieu increasingly hostile to Vichy, he joined early in 1942 a new underground literary review, *Confluences*. He moved with Andrée to Chavannes-sur-Reyssouze, 100km from Lyon, in order to write a novel, quoting Stendhal in Venice in 1815: 'rien de ce qu'on fait ici ne peut me toucher; je suis passager sur le vaisseau' (*28*, p.72). In November, with the nazi occupation of the southern zone, *Paris-Soir* was scuttled, severely reducing Vailland's income. In January 1943, the 'passenger' became crew: a young communist *résistant*, Jacques-Francis Rolland (the Rodrigue of *Drôle de jeu*), in need of a safe house, came to stay, and Vailland was galvanised into action for the Resistance. He asked Rolland to transmit his application to join the clandestine PCF, and spent six weeks in a clinic in Caluire to be detoxified. Until June 1944, he was constantly on the move between Lyon and Paris. At the end of 1943, the death of Vailland's father led to a family crisis over the estate (*34*, p.279); Vailland was convinced that he had broken completely with his mother, but: 'elle a commencé à hanter ses cauchemars. Il la voyait en sorcière' (Geneviève Vailland, *34*, p.280). In the Resistance, he became *chef de réseau* in a Gaullist group in October 1943. Keen to see more direct action (*34*, p.299), he became leader, in January 1944, of the 'groupe Marat' (*34*, p.300), writing to his sister that 'toutes mes contradictions intérieures se sont résolues depuis deux ans ou sont en train d'achever de se résoudre' (*29* p.303). The narrator in *325 000 francs* writes in similar terms: 'L'écrivain arrivé à maturité a résolu ou surmonté ses conflits intérieurs' (*6*, p.33). After numerous arrests within his network, Vailland became a wanted man. In March, alone in the Paris flat of his superior in the Resistance,

Daniel Cordier ('Caracalla' in *Drôle de Jeu*), he chanced on a copy of Stendhal's *Lucien Leuwen*, and took it away with him: 'lecture sans discontinuer jusqu'à 5 heures du matin, avec par moments des cris de joie' (*28*, p.90). Of all Vailland's literary passions, that for Stendhal (1783–1842) was perhaps the most constant: as a novelist, as a master of clear style and psychological realism, as a lover of Italy, as an opponent of the Prussian and Austrian victors of 1815 and their allies in France, and as a man in pursuit of happiness. He immediately wrote the first thirty-five pages of his first novel, *Drôle de Jeu* (*34*, p.306), and in June, announcing to Rolland: 'je m'en vais' (*34*, p.308), he returned to Chavannes; his novel was finished by September. In October he became a war correspondent for *Action* and *Libération*, following the allied armies. At the end of 1946, he decided to break with drugs and to spend the first half of 1947 with Andrée, writing his next novel. When the two projects proved incompatible, he broke once and for all with drugs and, in July, with Andrée. His next novel, *Les Mauvais Coups* (1948), is the story of the last stages of the relationship between Milan and Roberte, who commits suicide at the end; more than ten years later, Vailland 'rêvait encore fréquemment à Boule [Andrée]. Dans ses cauchemars elle l'étranglait avec des serpents et prenait parfois le visage de sa mère' (*34*, p.840). Andrée committed suicide in 1962.

In 1949, living in Sceaux, in the southern suburbs of Paris, and selling Communist newspapers and periodicals on the streets, Vailland made his first contacts with working-class people, and adopted with sectarian zeal the 'line' of a Party of which he was still not a member. He began his third novel, *Bon pied bon œil* (1950), setting some of the characters of *Drôle de Jeu* in the Cold War period, and met Lisina (Elisabeth) Naldi, who was to become his second wife. In December 1950 he embarked on a journey to Indonesia as a *grand reporter*. Returning to France to begin his new life with Elisabeth, he found that he was unable to resist the temptations of Paris; they moved in the Spring to spartan accommodation outside the hamlet of Les Allymes, near the point of intersection of la Bresse, le Bugey and le Jura. At Ambérieu-en-Bugey station, they met Henri Bourbon, who had resumed his railway job after five years as a PCF *député*. If from 1951–56 Vailland worshipped Stalin from afar, he formed a deep personal attachment to Bourbon, who was the opposite of a party apparatchik. In May 1952, at the height of the Cold War, his play *Le Colonel Foster plaidera coupable*, set in the Korean War, was banned as a 'spectacle de nature à troubler l'ordre public',[1] after the first performance had been brought to a halt by right-wing demonstrators; the police, using tear-gas, evacuated the theatre. In June, Vailland dramatically sent his application to join the PCF to Jacques Duclos, the Party deputy leader, who had been imprisoned on a trumped-up spying charge. By joining the PCF Vailland, according to Article 2 of the statutes, 'adhère à l'une des organisations de base du Parti, s'engage à y militer activement' (Fonds RV[2]). For the next four years, he did just that, writing for newspapers and periodicals close to, or run by, the PCF, often as a contribution to political and industrial campaigns. In 1953 he used the local textile industry, which he had just investigated in a series of four articles (*27*, pp.170–92) as the setting for his next novel, *Beau Masque*. A sequence of events in early 1954 illustrates the nature of Vailland's relations with the PCF, at national and at local level: asked by *L'Humanité* to write a dramatic text for the newspaper's fiftieth anniversary celebrations, he refused, saying that he could not afford to delay finishing *Beau Masque*. The PCF then contacted Bourbon, who asked Vailland personally. Vailland accepted; a fortnight later, *Batailles pour l'Humanité* was ready. In August 1954, after his divorce from Andrée, he moved with Elisabeth to Meillonnas (where Bourbon and his wife had recently moved), twenty kilometres from Bourg en Bresse; they were married in October. The following year, the writing of his next novel, *325 000 francs*, was also interrupted for the sake of *L'Humanité*, when he went to Lorraine to cover a strike at a steelworks. As a result of an article (Fonds RV) describing the aftermath of a charge by the CRS riot police, he was charged with 'complicité de diffamation

---

[1] *Le Monde*, 20 May 1952.
[2] For details of the Vailland archive in Bourg en Bresse, see the Select Bibliography.

publique envers une administration publique', and convicted in November 1956 (Fonds RV). Towards the end of 1955, extracts from *325 000 francs* were due to appear in *L'Humanité-Dimanche*, but were replaced by extracts from Aragon's latest novel. A congratulatory letter on *325 000 francs* from the Party leader Thorez smoothed Vailland's ruffled feathers, and he threw himself into Bourbon's successful campaign for re-election as a *député*. He was fired by enthusiasm for a new novel centring on a professional revolutionary, but emphasising 'la solitude du communiste quand il est vraiment à l'avant-garde, l'avant-garde est par définition seule' (*28*, p.475).

Then everything changed for Vailland. After the first reports had reached France of Khruschev's secret speech to the twentieth Congress of the Communist Party of the USSR, denouncing Stalin's crimes, Henri Lefebvre brought to Meillonnas a copy of the text of Khruschev's speech: 'Lefebvre avait beau lui dire: "Tout est vrai", Vailland se refusait encore à le croire' (*34*, p.655). Meanwhile, Vailland found himself at odds with the PCF leadership over the Algerian crisis: on 18 April, he wrote (for the last time) the minutes of a meeting of the Meillonnas cell of the PCF; the meeting 'estime que le vote des pleins pouvoirs [to the left-centre government under Guy Mollet] par le groupe communiste est contradictoire avec la prise de position du Parti Communiste contre la guerre d'Algérie' (Fonds RV). Taking up an invitation to attend the Czech writers' congress in Prague, Vailland went on, at the end of April, to Moscow, and came face to face with the evidence of Stalin's crimes. On returning to Meillonnas, he took down the portrait of Stalin, and chalked on his 'tableau noir à citations': 'Il n'y a plus rien au cœur de ma vie' (*34* p.661). Yet, like Marat in *Drôle de Jeu*, he had known what was at stake: 'La résistance [...] est essentiellement une longue promenade solitaire [...], qui mène — *malheur à moi s'il n'y mène pas* — qui mène au grand jour de sang où seront lavées toutes les hontes' (*1*, p.66; italics added). Marie-Louise Mercandino, staunch CGT and PCF member, and the inspiration for Pierrette Amable, the heroine of *Beau Masque*, concludes: 'Il avait placé trop haut le Parti, trop idéalisé Staline et le bolchevik' (*34*, p.661). Vailland created Resistance heroes in *Un Jeune Homme seul*, and working-class heroes in *Beau Masque*; but in *325 000 francs* there are no heroes: the journalist's eye and the novelist's imagination already reflect a reality which Vailland the man finally acknowledged in 1956: 'On se croit à l'extrême pointe de son temps et l'on réalise soudain que l'Histoire est entrée dans une nouvelle phase, sans qu'on s'en soit aperçu' (*28*, p.486). M. L. Mercandino's friendly reproach fell on deaf ears: 'Si tous les écrivains communistes nous abandonnent et qu'il n'y a plus que les pauvres diables pour se battre, ce n'était pas la peine de s'engager!' (*34*, p.661). Several intellectuals, including Marguerite Duras, Edgar Morin, J. F. Rolland and Claude Roy, broke publicly with the PCF over its refusal to acknowledge, let alone accept, the Khruschev report; others, including Henri Lefebvre, attempted to challenge the PCF line from the inside. The PCF's support in November 1956 for the crushing by the USSR of the Hungarian uprising led to a further series of departures, many 'sur la pointe des pieds': among others, François Furet, Annie Kriegel and E. Le Roy Ladurie. Vailland renewed his annual PCF membership until 1959, but took no further part in any of its activities or campaigns; later, he described his membership as having run from 1952 to 1956 or 1957 (*27*, p.498 and *28*, p.822). He avoided public criticism of the PCF; in his Journal, he shows sympathy for Bourbon in his personal and political difficulties (*28*, pp.623, 626–27; but see also p.661), but the tone is sharper towards members of the national PCF leadership (*28*, pp.573, 655, 673, 753 and 802).

1956 thus joins 1929 and 1947 as one of the years of decisive breaks in Vailland's life. This time, however, the break was neither an exclusion imposed on Vailland (as in 1929), nor a calculated decision on his part (as in 1947): external events were the catalyst for the collapse of an unsustainable vision of the world and of his place in it. His next novel, *La Loi*, provides, like *Beau Masque* and *325 000 francs*, a close study of individual characters within a specific social setting, this time in Italy (Apulia). His last two novels, *La Fête* (1960) and *La Truite* (1964), on the other hand, have their origins in personal preoccupations. The circular construction of *La Fête* recalls the closed world of Bionnas in *325 000 francs*, as does the opening scene of *La Truite*: 'je vois le bowling comme le ventre de la baleine; nous sommes dedans [...]; nous ne sortirons jamais du bowling' (*9*, pp.35–36). The real world, still magnificently present and alive in *La Loi*, merges in *La Fête* and *La Truite* with the novelist's dreams and obsessions. For Vailland, immobility is never far away, notwithstanding the bold claim made by Duc, Vailland's *alter ego* in *La Fête*: 'Il faut dégager à temps. Sinon, l'amour fou se change en tyrannie, subie ou imposée; le cocon qu'on tisse avec la drogue et qui protège du monde comme le ventre d'une mère, devient une prison [...]. Il a évité cela. C'est l'art de vivre' (*8*, p.217). In reality, Vailland was acutely aware of his predicament: 'Je fais ce que je veux. Tout ce que je veux. Et je m'englue dans le confort. Je voudrais me battre. Mais je ne sais plus contre qui me battre. On ne peut pas faire la guerre pour l'unique plaisir de retrouver la fraternité du combat' (*34*, p.814). After 1947, Vailland kept clear of drugs; but up to 1951 and increasingly from 1957, he drank to excess; he was a habitual smoker, and died of lung cancer in May 1965.

2. Fiction and social reality before 1960

In the nineteenth century, the increasing wealth and numerical strength of the middle classes produced a reading public for fiction and poetry where the working class appeared, if at all, in the vaguely menacing guise of 'le peuple', or in the shape of reassuringly worthy artisans and workers. In the latter part of the century the cumulative effect of the political, economic and social changes since the Revolution was to reveal that two groups, the middle class and the working class, now occupied the stage of History. Moral outrage at the injustices suffered by the lower orders of society had increasingly to contend with the practical question of whether promotion of the interests of the working class was harmful to the middle class, or whether it offered the best means of ensuring social stability and middle-class security.

Parallel to this political debate was the question of how the working class should be portrayed in literature. By the end of the nineteenth century, a solid body of works existed depicting everyday life in realistic terms, from the novels of Balzac, Hugo and Sand to the explicitly Realist novels of the Goncourt brothers, the polemical works of Vallès and the Naturalism of Zola. Observation of working-class life, however, necessarily entailed the portrayal of realities which many might find politically and personally unpalatable; the writer could justify this as being 'true to life' whatever the political implications, or as a spur to political action by and on behalf of the oppressed class. Zola advanced both of these arguments in defence of his novel *Germinal* (1885), warning the middle classes to heed the plight of the working class as the best means of warding off revolution. The working class thus emerged in literature as a class protagonist at the same time as it was becoming legitimised in society as a participant in economic and political affairs. The introduction, from 1881, of free, universal and compulsory elementary schooling made it theoretically possible for workers to have direct access to literature as readers, and enabled a few writers with working-class origins to add their voice to twentieth-century French literature.

The cataclysmic watershed of the First World War (1914–18) gave rise to a number of novels directly reflecting the experience of war for the ordinary soldier, among them Henri Barbusse's *Le Feu* (1916) and Roland Dorgelès's *Les Croix de bois* (1919). Their content and presentation were controversial, but they could not be condemned on the grounds of lack of truth to life. The immense impact of Barbusse's novel was instrumental in shaping and maintaining the conviction, widespread in France throughout the 1920s and 1930s, that another war had to be avoided at all costs; when Barbusse died in 1935, more than 300 000 people followed his coffin.

Civilian life in France among what was still called 'le peuple' was portrayed, more or less combatively, in novels such as Louis Guilloux's *La Maison du peuple* (1927) and Eugène Dabit's *Hôtel du Nord* (1931), respectively, but their authors were not necessarily writing within a specific theoretical or ideological framework. In the 1930s, however, a new doctrine emerged, originating from the USSR, and addressed directly to writers who protrayed the working class and its organisations. This was 'socialist realism', which explicitly linked the predominant mode of writing of the preceding decades (realism) to overt political aims (socialism). (For an account of the beginnings of socialist realism, see *43*, pp.98–108.) The resultant debate was wide-ranging, but had limited impact. Novels by left-wing writers as different as Paul Nizan (*Antoine Bloyé*, 1933) and Louis Aragon (*Les Cloches de Bâle*, 1934) were hailed by some as exemplars of socialist realism. After 1933, with the rise of fascism and the triumph of nazism, the Party line (in Moscow and then Paris) sought to include all 'progressive' writers as potential allies. In the 1930s, the dominant part played in Europe by political ideology, and the consequences of this, are reflected in the pro-Republican stance of André Malraux's *L'Espoir* (1937), set in the Spanish Civil War, and the pro-fascist stance of Robert

Brasillach's *les Sept couleurs* (1939), set in mid-1930s France and Germany. In France, after defeat and occupation, the search for unity in the Resistance, and victory against nazism and fascism, briefly provided the conditions for an inclusive, non-doctrinal approach to literature. Covert collaboratonists kept their heads down, and 'Resistance novels', such as Vailland's *Drôle de jeu* (1945) and Jean-Louis Curtis's *Les Forêts de la nuit* (1947) found favour on their own merits (as well as on their subject-matter), without being subjected to an additional ideological test.

Soon after 1945, however, the Cold War between the USA and the USSR brought with it widespread fears of a third World War, invasion and nuclear annihilation. In France and Italy, countries with a vigorous cultural and intellectual tradition, and where the Communist Party gained between a quarter and a third of votes cast in national elections, the polarisation of debate on public issues was intense, reaching a peak between 1948 and 1952. The subtlety of sincerely held positions counted for nothing; inexorably, writers, and above all specific works of literature were allocated to one or other camp, and many publications and organisations were covertly financed either by Moscow or by Washington. In this atmosphere, pro- and anti-communists watched to see which way the other side would jump. This happened in 1948 with Sartre's play *Les Mains sales*: when it was declared 'anticommunist' in the PCF press, the right-wing press hailed it as 'pro-freedom'. From 1947 to 1956, and to a lesser extent thereafter, the PCF, following Moscow, attempted to develop (although with limited impact) a theoretical, even scientific basis for socialist realism as an instrument for evaluating works of art and literature, in order to foster literary production consistent with the ideology and cultural policy of the PCF. This was the intellectual and political climate in which *Un Jeune Homme seul* and *325 000 francs* were written. (For an account of this theory, the PCF's cultural policy and Vailland's position, see *39*, pp.368–405 and *40*, pp.96–102.)

Much of the argument for the scientific basis of socialist realism was conducted in terms of the opposition between form and content: the writer's function was to provide the form through

which a particular content — the Party's ideology and policy —
could be expressed. The fundamental conflict, however, arises from
the tensions between the very nature of fiction, which is rooted in
the mutually supportive freedom of writer and reader, and
ideological commitment, with its concomitant pressures to prejudge,
underline and conclude. For example, the theory allowed for private
lives and 'personal problems' to be part of the content of novels, but
in practice the Party frowned on any representation of human
behaviour, particularly of sexuality, which might show the working
class in an unfavourable light. The result was that 'les questions
posées à l'individu dans les romans du nouveau réalisme conduisent
toujours à des réponses *politiques*. Les personnages de ces livres,
parce que réduits à être des *arguments*, disposés selon des règles en
vue d'une démonstration, ne sont que des exemples de "personnes
sociales typiques"' (*39*, p.377). Novelists who chose the communist
cause found themselves drawn into the straitjacket of socialist
realism: in the first volume of *Le Premier Choc* (1951), André Stil
shows communism as the only viable alternative; *La Place rouge*
(1961), by Pierre Courtade, is an account of one man's political
education between 1935 and 1958. Only Aragon, from his
unassailable position at the summit of the PCF's intellectual
hierarchy as a member of the Central Committee, was able to escape
this dilemma, whether through the looking-glass of history (*La
Semaine Sainte*, 1958) or, eventually, by abandoning realism,
socialist or otherwise (*La Mise à mort*, 1965).

The collapse of the Soviet empire in 1989–91 removed a point
of reference which had shaped much of the political debate, and
coloured the cultural climate, in western Europe since 1945. Today,
the attempts to establish a theory and practice of socialist realism
are of largely historical interest. Although the PCF was one of the
last European communist parties to embrace — or to have been
embraced by — cultural pluralism, by the end of the twentieth
century, the conversion appeared complete. Welcoming with
enthusiasm the publication of a new edition of Vailland's last
article, 'Eloge de la politique' (*28*, pp.804–09) Roland Leroy,
formerly director of *L'Humanité* and member of the Central

Committee of the PCF, affirms: 'Loin de moi l'idée de faire dire à Vailland plus qu'il n'a écrit. Je pense profondément comme il le disait (à propos du peintre Soulages): "Laissons les messages aux prophètes et aux facteurs" '.[3]

Vailland stands outside the theoretical debate within the PCF on socialist realism. In an essay of October 1951, 'De l'amateur', he insists that 'un roman ennuyeux est toujours un mauvais roman' (*24*, p.129). The essay ends with a dialogue which acknowledges socialist realism as an issue, but rejects the primacy of content over form: '— l'art réside dans la *manière*. / — Alors vous êtes contre le réalisme socialiste? / — Je suis toujours pour le réalisme quand on l'oppose à l'académisme comme la vie à la mort. Mais les socialistes n'ont pas encore eu le temps de broyer assez de couleurs pour s'apercevoir que ce qui est réel, ce n'est pas le modèle c'est la peinture' (*24*, p.132).

Vailland's less than orthodox conception of socialist realism, stressing the necessity of both form and content, and asserting the primacy of the specific contribution of the individual writer, stems from the intensely personal nature of his commitment in the early 1950s. Nevertheless, when he asserts in 1951 that 'Jamais un de mes amis communistes n'a essayé sous quelque forme que ce soit de me plier à une consigne quelconque' (*28*, p.450), he overlooks firstly that he had been prepared to accept a 'commande' from François Billoux, 'considéré comme le numéro trois du PCF' (*34*, p.460), for an essay on 'L'impérialisme Vatican contre la paix', published in 1978 as *Le Saint Empire*, secondly that the PCF did not publish this essay ('C'était une époque où les communistes tendaient la main aux catholiques', *34*, p.479), and thirdly that there was little need for him to be given instructions as to how he should write, since he saw suggestions (such as those made by Bourbon between the two drafts of *325 000 francs*: see below, *4.2*) as helping him to achieve his own objectives, as well as those of the PCF. Indeed, some of the PCF hierarchy in Paris may well have felt that Vailland would have been of more use to them as a communist sympathiser or 'fellow-traveller' than as a Party member, in

---

[3] *L'Humanité*, 29 September 1999.

supporting campaigns such as the Mouvement de la Paix (1952–57). By applying for his Party card in the circumstances of June 1952, Vailland had, to some extent, forced the Party's hand.

Vailland's commitment to the PCF from 1950 to 1956 provides him, as a writer, with a target audience, but not with a blueprint, whether theoretical or ideological. Indeed, Petr declares that '*Beau Masque* et *325 000 francs* ne sont en aucun cas, ni financièrement, ni intellectuellement, des œuvres de commande' (*39*, p.393). The characters in both novels are not mere ciphers or arguments, but original creations. Readers who prefer their realism bourgeois will naturally expect novels such as *Beau Masque* or *325 000 francs* to 'contain' communist or left-wing propaganda: 'Roger Vailland, qui aurait pu être un grand écrivain, ne rédige plus que vains et tristes tracts de propagande',[4] or :'Un roman comme *Beau Masque* ou comme *325 000 francs*, montre quel amas de principes et de consignes le "Parti" fait peser sur l'imagination des écrivains, même sur une imagination aussi capricieuse de nature'.[5]

It is precisely the weight of personal, psychological and mythological factors bearing, consciously and unconsciously, on the characters and actions of these novels, which puts them at a distance from the tenets of socialist realism. In *Un Jeune Homme seul*, the social setting is presented chiefly in terms of its significance for one individual character, Eugène-Marie, whose need for inclusion in a group which he finds more prestigious than his own family is stronger than any ideological commitment. In *Beau Masque*, the two main characters, particularly Pierrette Amable, are mythologised and individualised: they are more than representatives of their class and background. The diversity of character and attitude among the workers is stressed. In *325 000 francs*, the story of Busard and Marie-Jeanne is invested with personal and mythological significance, with the result that Busard's decline and fall illustrate simultaneously Vailland's view of male-female relationships and his sense of alienation from an inward-looking, unheroic society.

---

[4] R. Fallet, *Le Canard Enchaîné*, 19 December 1955.
[5] R. Poulet, *Rivarol*, 6 February 1969.

Since all three novels are rooted firmly in social reality, the reader is free to analyse and respond to events and characters as if they were real. Personal and mythological elements are put to the test of external reality; political, social and historical issues are presented from an identifiable individual standpoint. *Un Jeune Homme seul* cannot be said to 'mean' that one becomes a hero by joining a Resistance worker's funeral procession and beating up a Vichy policeman, any more than *325 000 francs* 'demonstrates' that Busard's selfish exploit is a less appropriate response to capitalist society than a lifetime spent negotiating and striking for marginal improvements in pay and conditions. Indeed, in the case of all three novels, Vailland was publicly and privately reproached for exposing the Party and its workers to charges of immorality and ideological weakness by including details of actions and characters deemed to be ideologically incorrect (see below, *4.2*). Whether these criticisms came from people who had espoused the cause of socialist realism, or from ordinary Party members or sympathisers, they illustrate the bankruptcy of socialist realism as a literary theory; they also suggest why it was that many of the novels for which it was claimed that they put the theory into practice were largely unreadable, and are unread today.

3. Un Jeune Homme seul

3.1 Un Jeune Homme seul *and external reality*

On 27 June 1951, Vailland set to work on the first novel of his new life. Under the heading 'R. V. lance un défi à Stakhanov / — Normes du roman' (Fonds RV), he kept a day-by-day account of the number of pages written. A similar chart accompanied the composition of every subsequent novel. In July he wrote to his mother: 'Je n'ai jamais tant et si bien travaillé' (*29*, p.310). For the subject-matter of his novel, he turned firstly to his feelings as an adolescent and young man (see below, *3.2*), and secondly to the period of Occupation and Resistance, which had formed the setting for *Drôle de jeu*, but which is treated in *Un Jeune Homme seul* from quite a different perspective.

The action of part 1 of *Un Jeune Homme seul* (pp.11–114) takes place during a few days in May 1923. The first five chapters (pp.11–64) are set in Reims, in and around the 'maison particulière' of Eugène-Marie's family; the last two chapters (pp 65–114) are set in Paris, during the wedding of Lucien Favart, Eugène-Marie's uncle, and Lucie Fleuri. For Eugène-Marie, the wedding represents his first real opportunity, at sixteen, to escape from the 'maison particulière' and the clutches of his relationship with his mother, and to have his eyes opened to the twin realities of politics and women, summed up in his encounter with the 13-year-old Domenica, whom he marries fourteen years later (p 128).

The action of part 2 of *Un Jeune Homme seul* (pp 115–200) also takes place during a few days: in April 1943, at a particularly dramatic and perilous period for the French Resistance. The structure of part 2 is more complex than that of part 1, with a flashback to a conversation between Eugène-Marie and Blanchette in July 1936 (pp.156–62). The action centres on Ste-Marie-des-

Anges, recognisable as Ambérieu-en-Bugey (see p.116), in the southern zone, occupied by the nazis since November 1942, but still divided from the northern zone. Marchand, Inspecteur principal de la Sûreté nationale, has come from Vichy to investigate a series of acts of sabotage in the area. The last of these has cost the life of Pierre Madru, a brother-in-law of Lucie Fleuri, and thus related to Eugène-Marie by marriage. Marchand questions Eugène-Marie (pp.118–24), the local police inspector (pp.125–30), the *patron* of a café (pp.131–32), and the Favarts' cleaning lady (pp.133–38). While Marchand is questioning Eugène-Marie a second time (having learnt a lot about his drinking habits and domestic situation), another explosion is heard: one of the turntables at the locomotive depot has been blown up (pp.139–42). In the next chapter, Lucien's brother Etienne Fleuri, of the Renseignements généraux, who has come from Paris for his brother-in-law's funeral, provides Marchand with some details about Blanchette, who made a brief appearance in part 1 (pp.78–79) as the mistress of a successful playwright. We now learn (pp.146–48) that Blanchette is a prostitute who had been Eugène-Marie's mistress. Summoned from Paris, Blanchette reveals many more details about her relationship with Eugène-Marie around 1936 (pp.153–64). The rest of the story leads chronologically to the set-piece of the funeral (pp.179–86), where Eugène-Marie joins the head of the cortege (pp.180–81), and the interrogation of Madru's son (pp.190–97), in the course of which Eugène-Marie finally 'voit rouge' (p.196).

The narrative perspective in *Un Jeune Homme seul* is the traditional one of a hidden narrator; the story, told in the third person, is centred on one character, the 'jeune homme seul'. However, the point of view changes between part 1, where everything is seen through Eugène-Marie's eyes, as if it were a first-person narrative, and part 2, where many scenes take place without Eugène-Marie's knowledge. The two-part structure of *Un Jeune Homme seul*, in which the wedding (in part 1) and Marchand's investigation (in part 2) are focal points, is dramatic and realistic, but not symbolic in the way that the structure of *325 000 francs* is symbolic (see below, *4.5*).

Un Jeune Homme seul brings within its scope a century of French history: from the birth of Victor-Emmanuel Servoz (p.83) to the present: 'un hôtel particulier [...] qu'on pouvait encore voir, en 1951' (p.66). The French defeat of 1870 and the Paris Commune of 1871 still resonate, somewhat uncertainly, in older people's memories (p.83): only Eugénie Favart (pp.92–94) is presented as giving a reliable account of events around 1870 (see below, *3.6*). The personal, social and political impact on French society of the Great War and its aftermath is shown, including the strikes of 1920 and the split at the end of that year between French socialists and communists. The characters are affected by, and respond to, public events or circumstances, such as the Front populaire in 1935–37, or the Occupation in 1940–44.

Part 1 of *Un Jeune Homme seul* spans middle-class, lower middle-class and working-class society, both provincial and Parisian. The stratification and compartmentalisation of French society provide the setting for Eugène-Marie's impatience at the restrictions of his provincial middle-class life, and his search for an alternative family. His desperate need to break out of his class is represented not only by his opposition to his parents, but also by the division between the 'maison particulière' and the outside world. From a window, he longingly watches and listens to the factory girls coming off their shift (p.57); he feels humiliated by his superior class position after the bicycle accident with a Polish worker (p.13).

In part 2, Eugène-Marie is still a prisoner of his class, but now the prestige of the working class in his eyes has been enhanced by its role in the Resistance. The funeral of Madru parallels the wedding in part 1, in that it brings together disparate groups of people, including Etienne Fleuri and his sister Jeanne, Madru's widow. But the dominant group is different: the vulgar *Ronde des cocus* (pp.83–87) is replaced by the respectful tones in which 'La foule faisait l'éloge du mort' (pp.184–85). Eugène-Marie's rapid conversion takes place in 1943, the year in which many people in occupied France changed sides, from accepting nazi occupation to resisting it.

Characters are situated within a specific set of family relationships and shown in their relation to social groupings; this contributes to the thematic unity and consistency of the novel. Personal characteristics are shown to interact with family and social forces: Eugène-Marie dreams of heroism, but while he remains physically and mentally within the confines of his narrow family, and of his mother in particular, his dreams and wishes are without effect. Only involvement in the actions of the real world can make a man of him.

Vailland creates a variety of relationships within and between two broad family groupings, the Favarts and the Fleuris, which come together through the wedding of Lucien Favart and Lucie Fleuri. Etienne Fleuri and his brother-in-law Madru are on opposite sides in 1923 (police – communist worker), and remain on opposite sides in 1943 (Vichy police – communist *résistant*). Significantly, the three principal positive characters in the novel are outsiders who marry into one of these two families: Eugénie Lajoux marries François Favart, Pierre Madru marries Jeanne Fleuri, and Domenica Dominguez marries Eugène-Marie Favart. Michel Favart is out of place in the Favart family; his son Eugène-Marie is equally out of place in part 1, and finds it at the end of part 2 only through committing himself to a cause which transcends his family. By setting the story of *Un Jeune Homme seul* at two or three key points in the history of France in the first half of the twentieth century, Vailland raises a number of issues: the isolation of the middle class from other sectors of the population, particularly the working class; the obstacles set by French society in the way of a young man seeking to combine personal development and social integration; the opportunity provided by defeat, occupation and resistance to overcome this isolation and these obstacles. These issues, which cover the period of Vailland's own life since adolescence, are viewed through the prism of his life in 1951. Some of the changes involving Madru and Domenica made in the course of writing the novel show these new external factors at work.

Details about Madru are modified, added or removed in order to enhance his political and personal stature. A conversation with

Servoz is reshaped so as to lead up to the conclusion that '— Le
capital français [...] veut exploiter jusqu'au bout sa victoire
militaire' (p.69). Towards the end of Eugène-Marie's conversation
with his uncle Lucien on the second day of the wedding (p.106),
Vailland deletes a question about Madru, and Lucien's reply: '—
Madru crève de faim, depuis qu'il a été révoqué'; '— Pour l'instant,
c'est sa femme qui bosse pour lui' (Fonds RV). Reflecting in part
Vailland's growing acquaintance with and admiration for Henri
Bourbon (see above, chapter *1*), these changes strengthen Madru's
role in the novel as a force acting on Eugène-Marie, and onto whom
Eugène-Marie projects his ideal of heroism. Indeed, Madru
eventually attains mythological stature: he dies a hero's death, in
action, and at his funeral his qualities and exploits are solemnly
celebrated by the people, in the manner of a Greek chorus (pp.184–
85). This mythological stature of Madru in turn lends realism to the
portrayal of Eugène-Marie, who is neither superhuman nor a
martyr: at the end of the novel, it is not stated whether he escapes
from prison, or dies at the hands of his captors (see also below, *3.7*).

Domenica evolves from 'une Noire d'Haïti' in the manuscript
of part 1 to the descendant of a line of Spanish democrats and
republicans: not for the only time in the 1950s, Vailland draws back
from portraying, for an important character in a novel, a non-
European. Similarly, in *Beau Masque* Vailland makes Beau Masque
an Italian immigrant, and not a North African, as he was in the
1952 fragment of a first version of the novel. This caution on
Vailland's part should be seen in the context of his work as a
journalist: in an article of July 1952 (*27*, p.227–30), entitled
'Dignité humaine' for the newly-created *Défense de la Paix*, he
gives a moving account of the funeral of a North African, married to
a French woman, and shot by the police during one of the anti-
Ridgway demonstrations in Paris. In *Beau Masque*, he shows the
wretched conditions in which immigrant Italian and North African
labourers live and work on electrification of a railway line, and
Beau Masque loses his job as a result of his attempts to organise
both groups of immigrant workers in joint action to improve their
conditions (*5*, pp.22–23). The North Africans' daily fear of racist

attacks and provocations is shown by 'un très jeune Algérien qui courbait la tête entre les épaules et jetait autour de lui des regards craintifs, comme s'il s'attendait à être passé à tabac, une fois de plus, par la police de la métropole' (*5*, p.234). Writing in *L'Humanité*, Vailland admits: 'J'avais d'abord pensé faire de Beau Masque un Nord-Africain; j'y ai renoncé parce qu'il subsiste encore tant de racisme, même dans la classe ouvrière, qu'il n'était pas raisonnable que Pierrette Amable choisît pour compagnon un Nord-Africain' (*27*, p.395). Somewhat disingenuously, in view of the preceding remark, Vailland adds: 'Je suis un peu surpris qu'aucun critique n'ait souligné l'aspect dénonciateur du racisme de mon roman' (*27*, p.395). In *Un Jeune Homme seul*, Domenica is more likely, as a Spaniard, to have encountered someone with Eugène-Marie's social background, and to have been in the Resistance, along with many refugees and exiles from the Spanish Civil War. Vailland's wish to reflect social realities overcomes the exotic attraction of giving Eugène-Marie a Haitian wife, and of showing Victoria Favart's shock when Eugène-Marie tells her what he's been up to (pp.76–77). In the manuscript, this part of their dialogue reads: '— Peut-on savoir ce que tu as fait? / — J'ai discuté métaphysique avec une négresse. / — Tu as… quoi?… quelle négresse? / — Une négresse dont le père est en prison pour avoir assassiné le tyran de Tahiti' [*sic*] (Fonds RV).

3.2 Un Jeune Homme seul *and Vailland*

What makes *Un Jeune Homme seul* a rich and lively mixture is the explosive nature of the tension between Vailland and his past. The original impetus for the composition of the novel was Vailland's need, when he had just made a deliberate break with his recent past, to exorcise deep-seated demons from much earlier in his life.

An indication of Vailland's preoccupations as he embarked on *Un Jeune Homme seul* is provided by a set of notes he made for 'Le parricide' (*30*, pp.98–105), a film script in two parts, set in 1934 and 1944. The central character, aged 12 and 22, is Gilbert Comte, showing the lasting influence of Roger Gilbert-Lecomte (see above, chapter *1*), whose physical characteristics Vailland transposes to

Eugène-Marie Favart (*36*, p.73). The 'vie étriquée, mesquine, morne de la famille Comte' is contrasted with 'la vitalité du peuple'. The father, a personnel manager in a factory, is rigid and authoritarian; the mother is 'obsédée par l'idée de faire oublier ses origines'. Apart from the emblematic piano which no one can play, there are very few details about the mother. Irène, Gilbert's cousin, aged seventeen, lives with the family following her father's death; Gilbert, through a hole in the wall between his room and his parents', learns that they had schemed to drive Irène away. Gilbert and Irène meet up again in a Resistance group: 'Grande passion réciproque'. The group is betrayed, and Irène is arrested. Gilbert discovers that the group has been spied on at the factory. A booby-trapped bomb is placed in the listening-post, but Gilbert discovers the 'TROU de son enfance', and learns that it was his father who had betrayed the group. At the factory, the father is affectionate towards Gilbert, who realises that it is his father's privileges, not his father, that he should hate. But 'Une affiche de propagande allemande rappelle à Gilbert les camarades torturés, dont Irène', and Gilbert lets his father go into the factory, to his death. The last two paragraphs of these notes are significant for their fusion of political and psychological values: Gilbert's contradicions have to be overcome 'par l'action, le combat (la Résistance, l'amour) pour qu'il devienne un homme [...]. C'est une *tragédie*. C'est Œdipe dans notre temps [...]. Gilbert ne peut devenir un "homme" qu'en tuant son père'. These preoccupations appear clearly in a short fantasy-tale written when Vailland was seventeen, *Les Hommes nus* (*13*): Eygurande, after murdering his father, makes love to a 'petite bergère impubère', but is hunted by armed militiamen threatening retribution. He takes refuge in the belly of an elephant from which he leaps out 'sanglant comme un nouveau-né', and makes his escape.[6]

In *Un Jeune Homme seul*, Eugène-Marie's father is 'executed' symbolically at the wedding, during the *Ronde des cocus* (pp.85–

---

[6] The theme of fraternity between prisoners also appears in a film scenario co-written by Vailland in 1949: see A. and O. Virmaux, *Cahiers Roger-Vailland 15*, June 2001, pp.139–40.

86), and his death in 1929 is mentioned only in passing (p.135); Vailland's own father died in 1943. It is as if sketching out 'Le parricide' enabled Vailland to exorcise his grievances against his father: the notes for 'Le parricide' are not dated, but in *Boroboudour*, written just before *Un Jeune Homme seul*, Vailland declares that 'le rapport père-enfants, qui constitue le fondement de la société féodale, est à l'origine de la plupart des psychoses décrites par la psychanalyse' (*25*, p.44). Despite this, as Picard points out, *Boroboudour* is 'entièrement dominé par l'obsession de la Mère' (*37*, p.27). Writing *Un Jeune Homme seul* brings Vailland face to face with the second part of Œdipus's tragic destiny. The figure of Eugène-Marie's mother Victoria dominates several passages in part 1, to an extent and in ways which do not correspond to the role played by Vailland's own mother in the family household, according to his sister Geneviève's account (*31*, pp.25–27 and *34*, pp.541–42); the savage portrait of Victoria Favart in part 2, which has no basis in reality, bears witness to Vailland's continuing struggle to free himself from a debilitating mixture of guilt and resentment against his mother.

Although the autobiographical elements in *Un Jeune Homme seul* therefore represent Vailland's internal history, viewed from a distance of thirty years, and not a direct portrayal of his own mother (or father), many details and scenes between fictional mother and son are transpositions, even transcriptions, of the real-life relationship. In chapter 3 (pp.28–38), there is the closeness and ritualised language between mother and son (pp.30–32), the mother's horror on learning that her son has called the Catholic schoolboys 'des petits cons' (p.35), her protective attitude ('On m'a sali mon enfant!', p.36) and the son's ambivalence about this. For the final version of *Un Jeune Homme seul*, Vailland deleted a large amount of autobiographical material concerning Eugène-Marie's family life and his relationship with his mother.

Eugène-Marie's mother is present in his daydreams about the factory girls: 'Eugène-Marie entrouvrit la fenêtre, pour entendre leurs voix grasses. Sa mère affirmait que si elles étaient toujours enrouées, c'était à cause des alcools qu'elles buvaient' (p.57). In the name of his sexual ideal, he rejects both his classmates' jokes and obscenities and the use of the word 'cochonnerie' by his mother (p.58). He goes to a brothel with a group of schoolfriends, but: 'Quand la fille du bordel [...] lui a dit: "Alors, tu te décides?" en lui posant la main sur la cuisse, son cœur s'est soulevé et il est sorti' (p.58). This contrasts with the earlier scene between mother and son: 'Il s'assit par terre, à ses genoux, les mains posées sur ses mains et le visage tourné vers ses yeux' (p.30); 'le garçon l'attira dans ses bras et la serra contre lui. Elle se laissa aller' (p.32). Instead of being an expression of masculinity (a sexual identity constructed on the basis of physiological differences between males and females), sexual activity becomes an assertion of virility (a capacity for sexual performance, which is always in question and thus has to be incessantly verified and asserted), against the ever-present danger of regressing to the initial duality of the mother-child relationship.[7] According to Elisabeth: 'Il voyait les femmes comme une épreuve. La femme qui était dans son lit représentait, comme il le disait, "l'objet qui devait susciter la performance virile"' (*31*, p.162). Vailland's vision of women is intensely polarised: they are objects of sexual desire and curiosity who, on acquaintance, intimacy and cohabitation, conjure up the all-powerful image of the Mother, and even of the womb from which he must escape in order to live. In *La Fête* (*8*, pp.226–27), Duc remembers a dream of pursuing a tall, apparently willing adolescent girl: 'Mais à la base d'un névé il s'enlisa dans la neige fondante [...] Il se réveilla en sueur, la bouche sèche, frappant du pied, de toutes ses forces, la terre, la neige et l'eau, la montagne, le ventre de sa femme, le ventre de sa mère'.

It is essential for the dramatic structure of *Un Jeune Homme seul* for the reader to believe that Eugène-Marie has the capacity to develop; it is therefore not surprising that Vailland deleted a passage which appears to rule this out: 'Toi je te connais bien. Tu as la même nature que ton père et que moi, tu es un tendre et un faible.

---

[7] See M. Picard, 'Le thème des mères chez Roger Vailland', *Revue d'Histoire Littéraire de la France 71/4*, July/August 1971, pp.638–61, and in particular pp.646–49.

Tu essaies de ressembler à ta grand-mère mais tu n'y réussiras jamais'. Similarly, changes to a scene in chapter 6 reinforce the idea that Eugène-Marie is capable of 'virile' conduct: in the manuscript, it is Marcelle who suggests to him that they take a walk, and who kisses him; in the final version (pp.97–98), these initiatives are Eugène-Marie's. This is more in keeping with his resolute state of mind and enhanced status, after his victory in the *épreuve* of the fight with Dédé (pp.94–96). Writing of the 'declaration of unreadiness' made by characters in *Drôle de jeu, Bon pied bon œil* and *Un Jeune Homme seul*, Tame (*46*, p.297), while acknowledging that 'These declarations appear to mirror faithfully the writer's own traumas during his life', sees Vailland's use of these traumas in these novels as providing an opportunity to show a character with a potential, given certain circumstances, for development.

Part 1 of *Un Jeune Homme seul* thus portrays the adolescent Eugène-Marie's sense of isolation, and his idealisation of anyone representing those aspects of the outside world with which he seeks to be associated. In part 2, Eugène-Marie is shown, in both 1936 and 1943, as still unable to escape from the consequences of his too-close relationship with his mother. In 1943, she shares his household with Domenica, who is active in the Resistance, while he, when everything around him is changing, is in a state of torpor and detachment, a habitual drinker whose offers of drinks to the railway workers (pp.127–28) are a parody of solidarity and fraternity. Eugène-Marie's relationship with Victoria has now turned from love to hate; ironically, he is protected by his mother's presence in the household from the possibility that his wife Domenica might be tempted to be unfaithful to him with Madru's son (p.130). Victoria has become a caricature of her earlier self, attempting to forbid Domenica to attend Madru's funeral (p.176), treating her son as if they were still in Reims (pp.176–77), and asking Domenica 'Vous ne seriez pas juive par hasard?' (p.177). Her mother-in-law (Eugénie Favart) arrives and sends her upstairs, like a child: 'nous avons à parler de choses sérieuses, ma petite-fille et moi' (p.178). In part 1, Victoria is associated with her possessions; in part 2, Blanchette says that sadism and masochism both arise from having possessions: 'Tout homme qui possède quelque chose, ne pense plus qu'à humilier ou à se faire humilier' (p.162). The theme of sadism reappears later in the novel, when Marchand boasts that he has an infallible method for making a suspect talk. Through the use of the usual term for this procedure, 'accoucher' (p.192), the association of sadism with the mother is maintained, along with the helplessness of the victim: 'se déculotter'; 'ils lâchent tout'; 'un lâche soulagement' (pp.192–93).

The heroic qualities which for Vailland are a touchstone of virility are frequently found in his female characters: positive Mother-figures who are invested with phallic power. Novels as diverse as *Les Mauvais Coups*, *La Loi* and *La Truite* express fascination with women who take the initiative, particularly in their relation with a man. In *Un Jeune Homme seul*, Domenica's virile occupations, in both 1923 and 1943, are contrasted with Eugène-Marie's unvirile preoccupations. Pierrette Amable, in *Beau Masque*, is more fully developed as a phallic character: in the eyes of the unheroic, degenerate Philippe Letourneau, 'Elle me faisait penser à une épée, elle est comme une lame d'acier (*5*, p.181). The narrator observes that 'elle a la main forte, un peu garçonnière' (*5*, p.232); Pierrette herself describes her shop as 'l'atelier *de fer*' (*5*, p.252). The novel concludes with the words 'Elle sera d'une trempe sans égale' (*5*, p.331).

For Vailland, as Picard points out, the couple 'ne peut exister comme tel que dans la mesure où […] l'épouse parvient à être à la fois une femme-mère (positive) et, mieux encore qu'un "double", une femme-frère' (*37*, p.423). In his first marriage, Vailland attempted to see Andrée as a positive Mother-figure, signing letters to her in 1940 as 'Ton "fils"' (*34*, pp.251–52). In his second marriage, Vailland cast Elisabeth more in the role of a 'femme-frère'; this is given fictional expression in *Un Jeune Homme seul* when, towards the end of the novel, Domenica plays the part of the ideal 'femme-frère', confident of Eugène-Marie's rise to heroic stature, and also in his portrayal of the narrator and Cordélia in *325 000 francs*, and of Duc and Léone in *La Fête*. Between these couples, the sexual element is not focused on: the ideal couple transcends male-female distinctions by removing from the male partner the anxiety of being alone and of needing to assert his virility vis-à-vis the female partner.

3.3 'L'homme le plus seul au monde'

Un Jeune Homme seul contains a series of illustrations of, and reflections on, the nature of solitude and ways of dealing with it. 'Solitude' has negative connotations whenever it is associated with Eugène-Marie's family in the 'maison particulière'. Within the context of the Savoyard or Resistance families, however, solitude is transformed (see below, *3.6*): these families enhance individuality by offering possibilities for individual action, through which strength of character is revealed by being put to the test ('l'épreuve').

The theme of solitude, in its negative connotations, is pursued throughout part 1, and for much of part 2. In the early stages of the wedding (pp.67–76), Eugène-Marie's response to being invited by his aunt and uncle to have a drink is to think that 'ils sont bons et délicats [...], comme s'ils ignoraient qu'il est condamné à la solitude à perpétuité [...]. Eugène-Marie se sent débordant d'amour pour la famille de Paris' (p.71). These feelings, however, do not outlast his sense of humiliation when Marcelle laughs at him for claiming that Etienne Fleuri, who works for the Special Branch ('la Secrète'), is not a policeman ('un flic'). He rushes back to his room and flings himself on the bed; 'Il répète à voix haute: "Je suis l'homme le plus seul au monde, je suis..."' (p.72). Enter the 13-year-old Domenica; but soon she too holds up a mirror to his solitude: 'Tu n'es pas intéressant [...]. Ni ennemis, ni maîtresse, qu'est-ce que tu fais dans la vie?' (p.74).

Already in *Drôle de jeu*, the theme of solitude appears, associated with the central character, Marat: for fragments of Marat's *journal intime*, Vailland uses autobiographical material: '*Lyon, 3 novembre 1940. — Très triste. En manque de B...* "L'homme le plus seul sur la terre"' (*1*, p.194); in September 1940, Vaillond writes to Andrée: 'Je me sens si loin de toi et si impuissant [...]. Je suis l'homme le plus seul qu'il y ait au monde' (letter to

Andrée, 15 September 1940, *34*, p.251). In *Les Mauvais Coups*, Milan reflects that 'il était l'être le plus seul dans le monde' (*2*, p.133). In 1950, Vailland writes to Elisabeth promising to look after himself: 'c'est normal puisque je ne suis plus l'homme le plus seul dans le monde' (*28*, p.325).

Vailland oscillates between seeing his sense of solitude as the product of specific circumstances, and as something fundamental to the human condition. In *Beau Masque*, during Pierrette's idyllic climb with Beau Masque through the bracken to the ridge where they make love for the first time, they see a kite (*un milan*) attacked by three (later ten) crows: '— Les corbeaux gagnent toujours, cria Pierrette. / — C'est parce qu'ils vont par bandes, cria Beau Masque. / — Les lâches, cria Pierrette' (*5*, p.125). This choice of the kite over the crows is fundamental to Vailland's conception of the only valid alternative to solitude, which is the full acceptance of and search for individuality, 'le singulier'. *Un Jeune Homme seul* can thus be seen as an attempt to delineate a worthy way out of bourgeois solitude, based on an ethic of individual development through action within, or at least associated with, a community which respects the individual and which the individual can respect.

3.4   'Une gifle fait voir rouge'

Although Eugène-Marie is painfully aware of his inadequacies, and has a burning desire to overcome them, willpower alone in *Un Jeune Homme seul* makes no difference. A spur is needed, a stimulus from outside which at last awakens the potential within the individual. This spur to action is symbolised by 'la gifle': titles Vailland considered for his novel include: 'Les trois gifles', 'Les exigences du sang', 'Un homme de cœur tue pour une gifle', and 'Une gifle fait voir rouge'.

The first 'gifle' in the novel is administered to Eugène-Marie's father, by his mother Eugénie Favart, when he fails the entrance examination for Polytechnique: 'Cette gifle, reçue et acceptée à l'âge de dix-neuf ans, avait décidé de sa carrière' (p.17; see also p.20). It becomes the point of fixation of Victoria Favart's resentment against both her husband and her mother-in-law: 'Et si elle te gifle, tu répondras encore une fois *amen*' (p.16); 'Moi, dit-elle, j'appelle cette lettre une gifle' (p.17); 'Chaque mot de ta mère est une gifle pour nous' (p.20). Eugène-Marie is sensitive above all to the humiliation involved in his father's acceptance of the slap (p.42). He writes down: '*Une gifle exige du sang*' (p.43), but the scene ends with him trapped by his father's kindness (p.52). At the end of chapter 5, he is beaten by his father for deciding to stop going to school: 'C'était la quatrième ou cinquième fois que son père le battait. [...] soudain, il avait cessé de reculer, relevé la tête et crié: "Frappe donc, grand lâche. Quand je serai grand, je te frapperai à mon tour et bien plus fort." [...] l'ingénieur-conseil était sorti de la pièce sans dire un mot et n'avait plus jamais touché Eugène-Marie' (pp.63–64). This scene suggests that Eugène-Marie has within him the capacity, when provoked, to assert himself against his circumstances. But within the family, within the walls of 'la maison particulière', nothing changes: '[il] avait cédé aux pleurs de Victoria, et était retourné le lendemain au lycée' (p.64).

Eugène-Marie's first public assertion of himself is when, at the wedding, he gets into a fight with Dédé over Marcelle, stung by Dédé's taunt 'Retourne dans les jupes de ta mère, fausse couche!' (p.95). But this is not the path of heroism: the next day, when Eugène-Marie tries to press home his advantage with Marcelle ('*Si je suis un homme, j'aurai Marcelle demain*', p.101), she resists him. He returns Dédé's insult by insulting her men friends, and suddenly 'déjà Marcelle le giflait' (p.113). His violent response is calmed down by the opportune arrival of Madru, who sets the record straight: '— J'ai vu rouge, dit Eugène-Marie. / — Une gifle fait voir rouge, dit Madru. Mais cette gifle-là, tu l'avais bien cherchée' (p.114). Madru has emerged as the replacement father-figure, who can divert Eugène-Marie's energies into more appropriate channels: associated with the communist Madru (and later with his son), 'seeing red' symbolises a political response, not an animal reflex. In part 2, an indication of the way forward is given by Blanchette, in her own pessimistic terms, when, in 1936, she telle Eugène-Marie that 'les ouvriers ne gagneront la partie que quand on les aura tellement battus qu'ils seront devenus méchants à leur tour' (p.162):

what matters is not the 'gifle' itself (of whatever kind and on whatever scale), but the response to it.

The final 'gifle' brings together the word's symbolic features. It occurs as a deliberate response to a repeated challenge in the form of an insult, given out to Etienne Fleuri by Madru's son: '— Toi, dit le gosse, t'es un sale flic de Vichy. / — Répète, dit Etienne Fleuri. / — Un sale flic! / Fleuri gifla le garçon à toute volée' (p.196). Eugène-Marie identifies totally at this point with Madru's son, and the ritual words apply to both of them: '*Une gifle fait voir rouge*'. All Eugène-Marie's past humiliations are gathered up, ready to be exorcised, in this one instant: 'Favart revit Madru, debout devant lui, dans l'arrière-loge de la concierge de la rue Pétrarque. Puis il vit son père, dressé devant la table du banquet de noce, son binocle à la main, *cocu, cu...*' (p.196). The essential response cannot come from Madru's son, who is still handcuffed: it is Eugène-Marie who now acts. In freeing Madru's son, he frees himself, and receives Madru's posthumous benediction through his son: 'Madru, murmura le gosse, avait bien dit que vous seriez un jour des nôtres' (p.197).

3.5 'Se défendre'

Refusal to submit to the humiliation represented by 'la gifle' thus offers the possibility of escape from bourgeois solitude, through heroism, to true individuality. In *Un Jeune Homme seul*, as in other novels (*Bon pied bon œil, Beau Masque* and, especially, *325 000 francs*), a heroic response is presented as exceptional. The most common response to suffering, humiliation and adversity is far less heroic, and is summed up in the term 'se défendre', associated with two characters in *Un Jeune Homme seul*: Eugène-Marie's uncle Lucien Favart (in part 1), and Blanchette (in part 2).

Lucien, who has married Lucie because she is pregnant, but who is not even sure he is the father, is wholly unheroic, whether as soldier or civilian, and he is not a communist. He says to Eugène-Marie: 'je fais comme tout le monde: je me défends... je me défends mal [...]. Je bricole' (pp. 105–06); 'Quand tout fout le camp, les hommes prennent peur et essaient de se planquer [...]. Etienne Fleuri s'est planqué dans la police; c'est sa manière à lui de se défendre' (p. 111). In 1943, Etienne Fleuri, who now takes his orders from the Vichy regime, uses the same expression when telling Marchand about Blanchette in 1914, when she was 25: 'elle se défendit mal, c'était une béguineuse, qui ne savait pas conserver un ami sérieux' (p.147). When Blanchette herself arrives in Sainte-Marie-des-Anges to tell her story to Marchand, the expression has a more specific meaning: 'elle avait été amenée peu à peu, et la vilenie des hommes l'y poussant, à se défendre sur les Champs-Elysées, puis aux Halles' (p.153). However, although 'se défendre' is associated with an unheroic way of life, 'ne pas se défendre', especially when one is socially or economically vulnerable, is presented as the worst of all possible attitudes. In *325 000 francs*, attempting to understand Marie-Jeanne's refusal of Busard, the narrator says to Cordélia: 'Marie-Jeanne se défend' (*6*, p.131). Juliette Doucet says to Busard: 'je me mets à la place de Marie-Jeanne. Elle se défend' (*6*, p.176). In 1956 Vailland writes of 'Marie-Jeanne', a neighbour in Meillonnas, that 'Elle a douloureusement appris à, comme elle dit, se défendre' (*24*, p.224).

In *Un Jeune Homme seul*, the theme of 'se défendre' is central to the discussion in 1936 between Blanchette and Eugène-Marie, who is pressing her to marry him (p.158). She refuses: 'Tu ne sauras jamais te défendre [...]. / — Les ouvriers savent se défendre, protesta-t-il. / — Non, dit-elle. Un ouvrier qui sait se défendre ne reste pas ouvrier, il devient patron' (p.161). In the manuscript, this sentence ends: 'Il devient patron ou larbin'; removing 'ou larbin' emphasises the political message. In *325 000 francs*, in a different context, 'être larbin' and 'être patron' are put on the same footing: Chatelard challenges Busard to explain why he wants to earn 325 000 francs, and Busard replies: 'Je me défends comme je peux' (*6*, p.106), whereupon Chatelard dismisses both alternatives: 'Etre larbin, voilà ton idéal'; 'Exploiter l'homme, voilà toute ton ambition' (*6*, p.109). As in *Un Jeune Homme seul*, the political implications of the issue are explored but remain unresolved.

The notion of 'se défendre' appears to hold a certain fascination for Vailland. In *Boroboudour*, he writes about his favourite flower: 'L'orchidée se défend aussi longuement que la

Présidente des *Liaisons dangereuses*' (*25*, p.53). At the end of *La Truite*, the narrator, Mariline and Saint-Genis are discussing Frédérique, 'vierge à vingt-quatre ans' (*9*, p.290): ' — J'espère, dis-je, que Frédérique tiendra. / Saint-Genis a ri. / — Qu'elle tienne, a-t-il dit, qu'elle tienne... mais pour quoi faire?' (*9*, pp.296–97). This celebration of flowers or women who are hard to get appears, with a change of sex, in *Un Jeune Homme seul*. Eugène-Marie is scornful of Marchand's claim that he knows how to make any suspect talk: 'Madru serait resté clos et intact devant vous' (p.193). The deep-seated fears and anxieties at the source of this admiration for a man or woman who remains 'clos et intact' are made to serve the novelist's purpose in *Un Jeune Homme seul*: in the manuscript, the discussion of Marchand's claim is longer and more detailed, and appears much earlier. Placed near the end of the novel, the exchange between Eugène-Marie and Marchand supports the implication of the prison scene (pp.198–99) that Eugène-Marie has not talked, and will not talk, under torture.

3.6   *The theme of the family in* Un Jeune Homme seul

In 1962, attempting to explain why two of his close friends have rejoined the PCF, Vailland writes: 'Les humains ont besoin de famille. Le "grand homme" seul est au-delà des familles, il ne peut plus appartenir à aucune famille. S'il est auteur de famille, elle ne peut légitimement que se dresser contre lui et il n'en est que plus seul (Staline, César)' (*28*, p.708).

What Eugène-Marie has to escape from, and what he has to attain, are both expressed through the theme of the family. The family that he has to leave, represented by his father and his mother, and their 'maison particulière', is the one that has made him 'l'homme le plus seul au monde'; the family that he has to find is, ultimately, a state of being. This is embodied on the one hand in his peasant, Savoyard origins, represented by his grandmother Eugénie Favart and on the other hand in the working class and the Resistance, represented by Madru and his son, and by Domenica. When his quest is over, Eugénie can at last say of him: 'Il a retrouvé les siens' (p.200); he will play his part in the Resistance and, one assumes, in the struggles of postwar France (see below, *3.7*).

In a letter of November 1951 to Pierre Berger, literary critic of *Paris-Presse* (*28*, pp.442–52), Vailland sets down at length his conception of the novel in general and of *Un Jeune Homme seul* in particular. However, when he attempts to clarify the meaning he gives to the words 'il a retrouvé les siens', his account exemplifies the impossibility of making a work of fiction carry a single concluding message. On the one hand, he rules out an exclusively communist interpretation of *Un Jeune Homme seul*, distancing himself from the claim by the French communists in 1951 'qui affirment être désormais les seuls défenseurs des traditions françaises' (*28*, p.449). He then endorses the Savoyard interpretation, but adds that 'A la correction des épreuves, j'ai failli modifier cette conclusion, par crainte d'un malentendu qui la ferait apparaître par trop barrésienne' (*28*, p.449). Vailland acknowledges, in order to reject it, the attraction he had once felt ('J'ai aimé Barrès', *28*, p.449) for the individualistic 'culte du moi' in the early writings of Maurice Barrès (1862–1923). Barrès's later espousal of fervent nationalism, rooted in Catholicism and his native Lorraine, could be seen, in 1951, as too closely associated with the 'Travail, Famille, Patrie' watchwords of the Vichy régime, and with right-wing, anti-democratic politics in general. (Vailland's earliest poems, in 1921, included several devoted to Joan of Arc: *34*, p.56.) The ideas of Barrès, which flow from a source deep within French sensitivity, also found expression in writers such as Bernanos or Mauriac, in the patriotic note struck by the Socialist leader Jaurès before 1914, and by Thorez and the PCF between 1941 and 1947.

The thematic structure of the novel, and the disposition of the forces within it, suggest that the two families represented respectively by Eugénie Favart and by Madru have an equal, mutually reinforcing potential for encouraging Eugène-Marie's heroic self-development.

The Savoyard family

As a sign of Savoyard origins, the name Favart has positive connotations: the dead grandfather François Favart, his widow Eugénie, and Victor-Emmanuel Servoz, who is related to her by marriage (p.77) are all Savoyard. Similarly, the Resistance family in *Un Jeune Homme seul* is composed, as it was in reality, of several different groupings: communists such as Domenica and Madru, the Christian trade unionist Roncevaux (p.127) and, among Eugénie Favart's Resistance contacts, a Gaullist group in Grenoble (pp.187–88).

Eugène-Marie's Savoyard origins are denoted in *Un Jeune Homme seul* by certain physical characteristics which formed part of Vailland's personal mythology, principally that of being tall and slim (see also *37*, pp.152–55); Vailland himself was thin, but not tall. In *Drôle de jeu*, Marat reflects that: 'Les grands montagnards maigres m'inspirent [...] immédiatement confiance; ce doit être héréditaire: je suis petit-fils de montagnard' (*1*, p.12). In *Beau Masque*: 'Les Amable sont grands et maigres, fortement charpentés' (*5*, p.13), and Beau Masque is 'De taille plutôt grande, maigre, la musculature très développée' (*5*, p.16). In *325 000 francs*, Jules Morel asks: 'Busard, c'est le grand maigre qui a failli gagner le circuit?' (*6*, p.91).

The first description of Eugène-Marie by an outsider comes in chapter 4, which is centred on Eugène-Marie's father. On seeing Eugène-Marie two years previously, the president of *l'Association des Savoyards de Reims* says of him: 'il est déjà aussi grand que son père et bien plus trapu que lui... et taillé comme les gens de Bonneville: si je l'avais rencontré dans la rue, j'aurais pensé: c'est un Favart' (p.46). Eugène-Marie's father is set aside as not coming up to the mark. As for his mother, she recognises Eugène-Marie's ancestry only to deplore it: ' "Il a déjà l'air plus savoyard que nature", ajouta tristement Victoria' (p.45). In the previous chapter, she says to him: 'C'est le sang des Favart qui parle en toi. On dit bien: Savoyard cabochard, Savoyard Favart double cabochard' (pp.34–35), and his grandfather Godichaux tells Eugène-Marie: 'Tu es fait du même bois qu'elle' (p.21), meaning Eugénie Favart.

At the wedding, it is Madru who introduces Eugène-Marie to Servoz as: 'le petit-fils de François Favart' (pp.69–70). Once again, Eugène-Marie's father is ignored as a link in the chain of generations. Fired by Servoz's account of his grandfather (p.70), Eugène-Marie eagerly questions his mother about him. Victoria insists on finding similarities between grandfather and father, bringing down the former to the level of the latter: 'le même regard que ton père quand il retire ses binocles [...]. Dans la vie courante il se laissait mener par ta grand-mère. En cela, il était comme ton père' (p.77). Eugène-Marie's curiosity about his grandfather, and his growing awareness of his Savoyard identity, are further stimulated by overhearing Victorien and Etienne Fleuri talking about taking him with them to a brothel: '— S'il a le sang aussi chaud que son grand-père le défroqué! [...] — A mon avis, il ressemble davantage au défroqué qu'au binoclard' (p.92). Eugène-Marie now questions his grandmother, and not his mother, about François Favart. Eugénie's detailed account (pp.92–94) provides Eugène-Marie with a complete pedigree: she says he is 'robuste et large d'épaules'; if he is not tall, 'C'était l'effet du sang auvergnat du grand-père Godichaux, mais le sang savoyard paraissait pourtant l'avoir emporté' (p.92). Eugénie also confirms that François Favart had been a *Communard* in 1871, as does Eugène-Marie's uncle Lucien (p.105). Vailland claimed repeatedly that his own grandfather had been a *Communard*; for an account of the facts as far as they have been established, see *34*, pp.12–13. The Paris Commune was not, of course, communist in the twentieth-century sense.

The living example of a true Savoyard is represented in both parts of the novel by Eugène-Marie's grandmother Eugénie Favart. Eugène-Marie's double name underlines the tension between his aspirations to heroism and virility, represented by his Savoyard grandmother Eugénie, and the dead weight of his conventional, effeminate, Catholic, bourgeois upbringing, symbolised in the name Marie (In *325 000 francs*, there is a similar duality in the name of Marie-Jeanne (see below, *4.3*). One could speculate whether Vailland's choice of name for Eugène-Marie feminises him; certainly the imperious Eugénie is invested with a host of 'masculine' qualities. Eugène-Marie imagines her as some kind of intransigent Jupiter (p.20). Eugène-Marie's grandfather Godichaux's account of her further underlines this masculinisation: '— Ta grand-mère, t'ai-je dit, était un roi. Elle donnait des pourboires comme un roi' (p.23). At her first appearance in the novel, at the wedding, she is 'Droite comme une jeune fille, *du temps que les jeunes filles savaient encore se tenir*' (pp.67–68). In part 2, now aged 85, 'elle se tenait aussi droite que vingt ans plus tôt' (p.177), whereas Vailland's paternal grandmother had died in 1930. Eugénie's first words, when she arrives unexpectedly at the house, only to find herself face to face with Victoria, are: 'As-tu des nouvelles de Domenica?' (p.177). In the funeral cortège, Eugénie and Domenica walk side by side, exchanging views on Eugène-Marie which express their different ages and standpoints, but which converge (pp.182–83). The two branches of Eugène-Marie's 'true' family, are shown to be of equal weight and value: '— Je lui fais confiance, parce qu'il est de bon sang, dit Eugénie Favart. / — Je lui fais confiance, parce qu'il aspire à la fraternité des hommes, dit Domenica' (p.183).

The Resistance family

The humiliating encounter with the Polish worker (pp.11–13) brings Eugène-Marie face to face with the barrier between him and the working class, underlined by his mother's acid comments about 'un *socialo*' and 'des *ouverreriers*' (p.31). It is not until the wedding, where he is confronted with several working-class members of his family — and with Domenica — that he realises the full extent of his ignorance, naivety and prejudices, as a result of his confinement in 'la maison particulière'. The first mention of Madru places him as the antithesis of Eugène-Marie's parents: 'Jeanne, vingt-trois ans, qui a repris le fer à repasser [...], depuis que son mari Pierre Madru, cheminot, a été révoqué à cause de son action au cours de la grande grève de 1920' (p.66). Madru's treatment of Eugène-Marie is, from the outset, paternal, benevolent, measured: when Marcelle makes fun of Eugène-Marie for his ignorance and naivety, Madru simply gives him the facts (p.72).

The thematic distribution of characters and actions is apparent at several points. Madru is distinguished from certain members of the Fleuri family: 'pendant le repas, Madru le cheminot révoqué, qui était fâché avec son beau-frère le policier, ne parla pas avec sa voisine de gauche, Rose la femme du policier' (p.81). Instead, he 'engagea par-dessus la table une discussion politique avec Victor-Emmanuel Servoz' (p 81). At the same time, the negative elements of the Favart and Fleuri families are brought together: 'Etienne le policier parlait à mi-voix avec Victoria, dont il partageait les points de vue sur l'éducation des garçons' (p.83). Then: 'Madru fit danser sa femme, puis sa belle-sœur Lucie, la mariée. / — Tu me fais danser? demanda Marcelle à Eugène-Marie. / — Je ne sais pas danser, dit Eugène-Marie' (p.90): only Madru is in his place. The personal and political distance between Madru and Eugène-Marie is underlined by Marcelle (pp.98–99); she adds that Eugène-Marie would look out of place at the public meeting Madru is due to address that evening, using the very word which Eugène-Marie had used as an insult to Dédé (p.96): 'ce sont les *tantes* qui se font faire des costumes comme le tien' (p.99). Thematically, this suggests that Victoria's influence on Eugène-Marie is devirilising, and that he must break free of it if he is to follow and approach the model represented by Madru.

On the second day of the wedding, Madru witnesses the scene between Eugène-Marie and Marcelle (p.113). Eugène-Marie moves to attack Madru, who imperturbably controls him until he calms down. Recanati points out that this scene is the counterpart to the scene where Eugène-Marie defies his father (pp.63–64: see above, *3.4*): 'Le transfert des pères ressort avec évidence du rapprochement des deux passages' (*31*, p.104; also *36*, pp.129–32). Madru's iron grip symbolises his authority: '[il] saisit les deux bras d'Eugène-Marie dans ses poignes, qui étaient de fer' (p.113), and his virility: 'Il regardait le garçon se contracter et frémir dans sa poigne de fer [...]. Madru sentit les muscles du garçon mollir. Il le lâcha' (p.114). It is as if Eugène-Marie has regressed from adolescence to childhood: 'Madru sortit. Eugène-Marie eut envie de courir derrière lui, de le saisir par le bras, de l'obliger à s'arrêter, à lui prêter attention, à l'écouter' (p.114). At the end of *325 000 francs*, Busard's artificial hand, described as 'Un instrument d'acier nickelé'; 'mi-pince, mi-crochet' (*6*, p.233) can be seen as the derisory antithesis to Madru's 'poigne de fer'. In 1963, Vailland makes this interpretation explicit: 'Busard, coupé de sa classe, veut faire la révolution pour lui tout seul'; 'Il y perd son poing viril et sa main de travailleur. Châtré et manchot' (*28*, pp.712–13).

In *Un Jeune Homme seul*, the label 'de fer' is used to emphasise the high and equal standing of Eugène-Marie's two ideal families, represented by Madru and Eugénie Favart. Towards the end of their first conversation, Domenica tells Eugène-Marie that her father and Eugénie knew one another: 'Il dit que c'est une femme de fer, qu'elle serait digne d'être espagnole' (p.76). Eugène-Marie notes this down as one of the highlights of the wedding (p.101). At Madru's funeral, the two ideal families are reunited, releasing Eugène-Marie's energies for decisive action. This time, he takes his place among them: Madru, he says to his grandmother, 'est le seul homme au monde que j'aie jamais respecté' (pp.180–81). Instead of wanting to run after Madru like a small child (p.114), he now walks behind Madru's coffin, like a man (p.181).

The theme of family is sustained, but with negative connotations, during the scene where Eugène-Marie is brought in by the police to help them put pressure on Madru's son, who has been caught red-handed, continuing his father's work. Marchand says to Eugène-Marie: 'c'est à une sorte de conseil de famille que je vous ai convoqué' (p.190). Of Madru's son, Marchand remarks: 'Il croit s'identifier aux héros que son père lui a donnés pour modèle, en résistant à mes paternelles adjurations' (p.191) — words reminiscent of Pétain, a *faux père* to the French people. But now, secure in his own new and publicy acknowledged identity, Eugène-Marie stoutly defends Madru's son, saying: 'Il n'a pas de vice [...]. Il se taira' (p.192), just as Madru had said to Marcelle of Eugène-Marie that 'Il est de bon sang' (p.114). Now 'le gosse' is not Eugène-Marie but Madru's son. All Eugène-Marie's words, for the rest of the scene, are words of action: 'Vite'; 'Tends les mains'; 'Tiens bon'; 'Passe le premier'; 'File' (p.197). Everything falls into place, and he acts as if he has been rehearsing for it all his life — which, in a sense, he has. This moment of swift, decisive action underlines the essential difference between the family that Eugène-Marie has left behind, and the family of which he is at last a part: within the former, he is doomed to be passive, isolated, undeveloped; whatever he is or does makes no difference. The new family, on the other hand, is a call to action, a challenge addressed to him as an individual: a place in this family has to be earned.

3.7   Interpretations of Un Jeune Homme seul

'Le thème habituel du théâtre javanais ou balinais est la lutte d'un jeune prince, un adolescent [...] contre toutes sortes de monstres [...]. C'est saint Georges et le dragon, la lutte des anges et des démons' (*25*, p.43). Vailland's words in *Boroboudour* prefigure the conceptual and mythological framework of his new novel. Writing about *Un Jeune Homme seul*, he uses the same image: 'je peins la lutte des héros contre les dragons'; 'saint Georges représente le progrès et le Dragon la réaction' (*28*, pp.443, 445–46; also *29*, p.311). In applying this notion to his novel, does Vailland deepen the reader's understanding, or is he in contradiction with his assertions (in October 1951) that 'l'art réside dans la *manière*'; 'ce qui est réel, ce n'est pas le modèle c'est la peinture' (*24*, p.132)?

The dramatic framework for *Un Jeune Homme seul* is provided by Vailland's long-standing admiration for the values and dramatic construction of Corneille's great tragedies. In notes for a lecture on 'Le héros de roman', given in January 1952, Vailland sees both plays and novels as accounts of a transformation: 'Une pièce de théâtre, c'est une *situation* qui, par les conflits qu'elle contient, se transforme; dans le roman, c'est le *héros* qui se transforme' (Fonds RV). From this Vailland concludes, in words that apply directly to *Un Jeune Homme seul*, that: 'tout grand roman est le récit d'une *métamorphose*. Les conflits du héros avec le monde et avec lui-même aboutissent au chapitre finale [*sic*] à sa métamorphose: il était un homme ordinaire, il est devenu un héros, un héros de roman' (ibid.).

Eugène-Marie is presented in part 1 as a bundle of emotional and physical energy, for which there is no outlet. He imagines how it would feel to be slapped as his father had been when he was nineteen: 'Quelque chose s'émut aussitôt au creux de sa poitrine […]. Cela lui coupa le souffle' (p.42). He analyses his feelings thus: 'Mes poings cherchaient quelque chose à frapper, se dit Eugène-Marie […]. Mes poings voulaient pénétrer, fouiller, faire saigner' (p.42). The dragon is shown to be lodged more within Eugène-Marie himself than within those with whom he jousts, be it his father, his mother or the likes of Dédé or Marcelle. For much of part 2 Eugène-Marie is inert, passive; as Petr points out: 'Ce que l'enquête du policier met progressivement au jour, c'est un décalage entre le temps *répétitif* de la vie de Favart et celui *dramatique* de la Résistance' (*39*, p.163). Domenica and Eugénie, discussing what they are to do next, see Eugène-Marie as someone they have to make allowances for. Domenica says: 'Il prétendra être encore rejeté hors de la communauté, si je ne lui demande rien. Je ne peux pas lui inventer une tâche, dans le seul but qu'il puisse se prouver à soi-même son courage' (p.188): words echoed by Vailland himself in 1959, in less exalted circumstances: 'On ne peut pas faire la guerre pour l'unique plaisir de retrouver la fraternité du combat' (*34*, p.814: see above, chapter *1*). For Domenica, his transformation is not complete: 'elle pensa […] qu'Eugène-Marie aussi, s'il se décidait à devenir un homme, s'exposerait volontairement à la torture' (p.189).

In the penultimate scene of the novel (pp.198–99), Eugène-Marie, after being beaten, is thrown, unconscious, into a cell with six other prisoners. This scene is remarkable for the air of tenderness which surrounds it; it is as if Eugène-Marie is being born into his new family: 'Sa tête était posée sur quelque chose de tiède et de vivant. Il entrouvrit les yeux, et vit que la cuisse d'un homme […] lui servait d'oreiller' (p.198). He looks at one of his fellow-prisoners: 'Favart regarda, entre ses cils mi-clos, les mains du petit gros, qui étaient longues et déliées comme celles de Madru' (p.199). This image of birth and/or rebirth, used elsewhere by Vailland when describing his 'awakening to life' on breaking with drugs in 1942, lends great power to the scene, which emphasises that Eugène-Marie's apotheosis, his (re)birth as a man, is possible only through individual heroic action. Without this, the benevolence of his mentors has no effect: he remains isolated, unborn. It is also possible to see this scene as an attempt to exorcise an incident from Vailland's childhood when, as a five-year-old, following a fit of rage at his mother at being reminded that it was time to go home for his baby sister Geneviève's feed, he was punished by being shut in a windowless box-room (*34*, p.22). There are few scenes of fraternity in Vailland's work: the focus is far more often on the individual; for once, at the end of *Un Jeune Homme seul*, Vailland asserts that the answer to solitude lies in individual action, which alone opens the gates to human fraternity. After living for so long 'à contre-temps', Eugène-Marie is suddenly enabled to achieve fusion between himself and his times, attaining heroic stature as an individual acting in support of the 'right' cause. It is at this level that the character of Eugène-Marie is autobiographical: the story of Eugène-Marie's self-fulfilment through decisive action, earning the approval of those he admires and respects, is also one of wish-fulfilment on the part of Vailland. This is particularly apparent in certain scenes, for example after Eugène-Marie has thrashed Dédé, 'ses yeux rencontrent les visages de Madru et de Servoz qui, du fond de l'atelier, le regardent avec un sourire bienveillant' (p.97), or at Madru's funeral: 'Les cheminots serraient la main de l'ingénieur, avec une intention particulière, qu'il traduisait: "Tu es donc des nôtres. Pourquoi ne l'as-tu pas montré plus tôt?"' (p.185). Although no indication is given in the novel itself of the eventual fate of the imprisoned Eugène-Marie, the element of wish-fulfilment involved in Vailland's identification with him as a hero in the making is confirmed in the 1952 fragment of *Beau Masque*, where mention is made of 'la gare de triage de Sainte-Marie-des-Anges, où Eugène-Marie Favart s'illustra en 1944, en faisant sauter 19 locomotives' (Fonds RV).

In the moment of transformation, personal doubts and inhibitions are overcome. The strong impression remains, however, that the would-be hero cannot himself create or even choose the conditions for his transformation, but is dependent on a combination of circumstances. Vailland's conception of heroism presupposes the existence of a period of time favourable to political action on the part of those with whom the hero identifies. Such was indeed the case for Vailland and the Resistance from 1942 to 1945; such appeared to Vailland to be the case for him and the PCF in the early 1950s. In reality, however, championing the USSR against the USA during the Cold War offered less certain and less exhilarating opportunities for heroism than the Resistance, particularly in view of the limited policy options open to the PCF in the 1950s. Despite this, Vailland succeeds in his next novel, *Beau Masque*, in placing a powerful story of heroism, resolution and sacrifice in a contemporary industrial setting; *325 000 francs*, however, is set in a world where there are few potential heroes, and still fewer opportunities for heroism.

4. 325 000 francs

4.1 325 000 francs *and external reality*

Un Jeune Homme seul culminates in a declaration of Vailland's commitment as a writer to the cause of those he regards as 'les siens'. *325 000 francs* can be read as one of the products of this commitment.

The wider implications of global capitalism, which form the backdrop and the impetus for much of the action in *Beau Masque*, are also present in *325 000 francs*. They influence the thinking and the actions of both Jules Morel, the owner of Plastoform, and of Chatelard, the union secretary: 'L'une des singularités de la France au début de la seconde moitié du XXe siècle aura été qu'aient travaillé dans la même usine, dans les mêmes ateliers, le Bressan qui pense sa tâche comme une magie, et Chatelard qui prépare une grève en faisant l'analyse du marché' (p.199). Busard, who has sold his labour to Jules Morel, eventually realises his insignificant place in the capitalist scheme of things (pp.159–60). In this respect, he is representative of his fellow-workers: 'En 1954, les données fondamentales des problèmes du travail, des prix et des salaires étaient familières à la plupart des jeunes gens des villes ouvrières' (pp.160–61). By and large, however, the people of Bionnas show very little preoccupation with wider issues, and have little or no control over the forces which shape their lives. In *325 000 francs*, the narrator says of Busard and Marie-Jeanne that 'Ils se trouvaient l'un et l'autre aussi ignorants des événements de leur temps que Paul et Virginie dans leur île. De telles singularités étaient encore possibles et même relativement fréquentes dans la France de ce temps-là' (pp.216–17).

The contradictions apparent in these 'singularités' (p.199 and p.217) arise as a result of post-war industrialisation and urbanisation, which had proceeded more slowly between 1850 and 1950 in France than in the USA, Germany, Britain or Belgium. In France, it was only in the early 1930s that the urban population outnumbered for the first time the rural and small-town population. Stimulated by the First World War and the Russian Revolution, the drive for mass production led to new forms of factory organisation and working systems: in the West, detailed time-and-motion studies of each stage of a production process in which each worker performed a fixed set of tasks, endlessly repeated; this system became known in France as 'taylorisme', after the American who had first devised it. In the USSR, the enforcement of ever-higher norms of production became known after 1935 as 'stakhanovism', after the name of the worker whose heroic achievements in surpassing the norm were hailed in propaganda as the example to be emulated by all Soviet workers. In the USSR and, after the Second World War, in Eastern Europe, this system survived for several decades. In the West, technological development and higher personal expectations of life and work had begun, by the 1950s, to challenge the 'Taylorist' system, and its claims to efficiency. In *325 000 francs*, the narrator comments on the introduction of a new, fully-automatic press in the Plastoform factory: 'voilà qui remplacera dans l'avenir le travail à la chaîne; les *Temps Modernes* de Charlie Chaplin ne seront plus qu'un témoignage du Moyen-Age de l'industrie' (p.153). The reference to Chaplin's satirical film of 1936 further undermines the human value of Busard's exploit: he has enslaved himself to a system which is about to disappear.

In 1950s France, the PCF had to compete with newly-awakened material aspirations centred on the home, the family and individual possessions; with its trade union ally, the Confédération générale du travail, it sought to consolidate its position in politics (particularly in local government) and the workplace. From these bastions, campaigns were mounted on national and international themes, and specific sectional and local issues. *325 000 francs* owes its origin to one such campaign. Faced with an unacceptably high incidence of mutilating accidents in the plastics industry in Oyonnax, Henri Bourbon suggested a campaign in the local

Communist press, with articles by Vailland. In June 1955, Vailland spent a week in Oyonnax, visiting factories and meeting workers; the local Party, union and press began to prepare a co-ordinated campaign. As a result of his investigations, Vailland conceived a different idea: 'cette affaire, ce n'est pas un article ou deux qui peuvent la régler. Ça peut faire plus qu'une nouvelle, moins qu'un roman, mais ça peut faire quelque chose d'extrêmement important' (quoted by Bourbon, *32*, p.22). By writing a novel instead of a series of articles for the Party press, Vailland could reach out beyond the limits within which the influence of the PCF had been contained since 1947.

A few weeks earlier, while covering, as a reporter for *L'Avant-Garde*, the principal east-European cycle race, the Course de la Paix, Vailland wrote to Elisabeth: 'La presse internationale annonce que je prépare un roman sur le cyclisme' (*28*, p.466). Certain passages of an article on the winner of this race prefigure material that appears in the first chapter of *325 000 francs*. A third external element in the conception of *325 000 francs* dates from the previous year, when Vailland stopped at a large snack-bar north of Chalon-sur-Saône and had the idea of writing a novel about someone 'qui aurait voulu s'en tirer tout seul' (René Ballet, personal communication, 1973). The characters, their preoccupations, their work and their leisure pursuits, are recognisably those of small-town France in the 1950s. Several fictional place names in *325 000 francs* (Bionnas, La Grange-aux-Vents, Le Clusot, la vallée de la Géline) correspond to geographical locations in the Ain *département* (respectively Oyonnax, Les Allymes, Nantua and la vallée de l'Albarine). Some local names are unchanged: Bellegarde, le col de la Faucille, Saint-Trivier-de-Courtes and Saint-Claude. As for the 'Circuit cycliste de Bionnas', no corresponding cycle race based in Oyonnax existed.

The external sources for several characters in *325 000 francs* were close at hand. Vailland had already written articles about the Bresse region, including the *fête des conscrits*; a young local farmer provided the details of le Bressan's physical appearance. A young working woman in Meillonnas, married to a long-distance lorry-driver, confided in Elisabeth; she dreamt of having, one day, 'un bistro pour ne pas être renfermée dans un trou' (Elisabeth Vailland, personal communication, 1973). Many details of her appearance and of her experience of men are given to Marie-Jeanne Lemercier, including her reason for not sleeping with a young man: 'J'en ai marre d'avorter' (ibid.). Similarly, Vailland made extensive use of conversations with Elisabeth for the dialogues between the narrator and his wife, Cordélia. Juliette Doucet is based on a young unmarried working woman in Oyonnax who rode around town on a scooter (scandalous in 1955), indifferent to gossip. She had none of Marie-Jeanne's caution about sex: 'je hais le patron, mais je m'en fous d'aller baiser avec lui si ça me donne de l'argent' (ibid.). Some details of Jules Morel are based on an Italian factory owner; Paul Morel resembles the son of a different factory owner. Chatelard is a composite character (in Vailland's notes, the names and brief details of ten other workers are listed) who is given some of the attitudes and expressions of Henri Bourbon, such as 'Tu dérailles!' (p.107).

Bionnas is a closed world from which there is no escape: this spatial image underpins the closed nature of the narrative as it unfolds in time (see below, *4.5*), and determines the interpretation of the novel as a whole (see below, *4.7*). It also constricts the personality and perspectives of the characters. Only the narrator and Cordélia are truly outside, even above Bionnas: 'J'habite un village de montagne, à peu de distance de Bionnas [...]. J'y descends souvent à la fin de l'après-midi' (p.5).

Busard's downfall is fully — perhaps over-fully — motivated; this contrasts with Eugène-Marie's sudden emergence as a hero in *Un Jeune Homme seul*. Busard is punished for overestimating his strength and resources, for having betrayed his class, and for having enslaved himself to Marie-Jeanne. Marie-Jeanne's perspective is entirely defensive: she has achieved some measure of security by offering the outside world as little as possible 'hold' on herself, but she is dependent on the goodwill of certain men (Jules Morel, Chatelard), and by consenting to marry Busard she makes herself dependent on his capacity to create a new life for them. When she declares 'Je veux quitter Bionnas' (p.69), she does not believe that it will happen, and she is proved right.

Le Bressan, by nature and through his socio-economic class, stands outside the closed world of Bionnas; his time in Bionnas is only an interlude in a rural life which is equally inescapable (pp.75–76). His brute strength and narrowness of vision mean that he can shrug off the pitfalls of the cycle race or of working at the press. He is, despite having no name to himself, a memorable character: 'J'aime le Bressan, personnage presque mythique. Il tient dans le roman [...] une place nettement plus importante que son rôle dans l'intrigue' (Sylvestre Faucon, letter to Vailland, 28 January 1956; Fonds RV). Juliette Doucet, as a young working woman, has some mobility, but her trips to Lyon or Geneva are paid for by Jules or Paul Morel. Like le Bressan, she is subject to specific socio-economic constraints. When she does leave Bionnas with a commercial traveller: 'Elle a déjà perdu l'éclat qui faisait penser à une montagne au printemps' (p.238). For the present, she is a living, moving contrast (p.13) to the immobility of Marie-Jeanne. Chatelard, the union secretary, has contacts with the world outside Bionnas, but his whole life is devoted to the defence of his fellow-workers. Reflecting the realities of industrial relations in 1950s France, the best he can do for his fellow-workers, even in a factory where the union is strong (p.214), is to use any changes in working practices to secure a modest pay increase.

Jules Morel, as owner of a factory, is as much subject to economic realities beyond his control as Chatelard is. Although Morel *père et fils* enjoy a certain mobility, they are tied to the factory as the source of their income.

4.2 Composition of 325 000 francs

While falling short of the Stakhanovite pace at which *Un Jeune Homme seul* was composed, *325 000 francs* was completed in three months. After writing a first draft, Vailland wrote: 'J'en ai marre depuis la main coupée' (Fonds RV), and was convinced that his novel was a failure (*33*, p.140). The final draft was completed in just over a month, ending with what he called a 'sprint au finish'

(Fonds RV). Vailland read the first draft to Bourbon, inviting him, as he had done for *Un Jeune Homme seul* and *Beau Masque*, to make specific comments and suggestions: 'Quand il avait écrit quelque chose qui n'allait pas, je le lui disais et, bien souvent, Roger modifiait sa façon d'opérer, de voir les choses. Pour *325 000 francs* notamment, je lui ai fait enlever deux ou trois pages qui pouvaient être interprétées contre nous' (Bourbon, *32*, p.15). Several of these deletions concerned the exploits of le Bressan during his *année de conscrit*, such as his sexual conquests (including a 65-year-old widow, and the wife of Jambe d'Argent) and details of the past adventures of the narrator and Jambe d'Argent. (For a detailed analysis of the changes Vailland made to *325 000 francs* in the course of composition, see *39*, pp.463–522 and 553–97.) Already, in *Un Jeune Homme seul*, Vailland removed from the final version explicit sexual details about Louise, Eugène-Marie's secretary (*4*, p.137), and about one of Blanchette's clients (*4*, p.156), and in the scene where Marchand comes to the café to sound out Eugène-Marie (*4*, p.150–51), Vailland removed two pages where Marchand talks graphically about finding out suspects' vices as a means of making them talk. The issue raised by such changes is not primarily one of censorship, still less one of slavish adherence to the tenets of socialist realism (see above, chapter 2). Vailland's intention in writing *325 000 francs* is clear: to produce a work of fiction which would have a wider and more lasting impact than articles in the regional press. In this respect, Bourbon's advice was sound; a letter to *l'Humanité* from a couple of communist primary-school teachers, after the serialisation of *325 000 francs*, illustrates the obstacles Vailland faced: 'Dans ce roman les gens du peuple sont présentés de façon erronée [...]. Les jeunes ouvrières couchent donc facilement avec le fils du patron [...]. En lisant ces romans [*Beau Masque* and *325 000 francs*], les réactionnaires auront beau jeu pour parler de la dépravation des travailleurs' (*34*, p.646). In the light of such a response, Petr's claim that 'Vailland supprime tout ce qui peut heurter la sensibilité puritaine des communistes français' (*39*, p.504) under-estimates the magnitude of Vailland's task.

Vailland's aim is also served by the changes, sometimes substantial, made on aesthetic and stylistic grounds, such as those affecting the rhythm and focus of the narrative. One example is the removal of references to some of le Bressan's more eyebrow-raising exploits: this lends coherence to imagery associated with le Bressan, making him not a bull, but an ox. A mention of le Bressan's boundless self-assurance is changed from 'Il se sentait fort à déraciner un sapin de vingt ans' (Fonds RV) to 'Il se sentait fort à obliger un bœuf à s'agenouiller devant lui' (p.76), and in a passage added to the scene where he gives Busard half the prize money he has just won, le Bressan says 'Nous sommes les deux bœufs de la même paire' (p.165). A further example is the threatened strike which, in the first version, is dealt with at length; at a late stage of composition, Vailland cut much of this out. This change safeguards the momentum of the novel and the focus on Busard, as well as high-lighting the economic knowledge and tactical sophistication of union leaders: 'Chatelard lisait attentivement les journaux professionnels français et étrangers [...]. Il venait ainsi d'apprendre que Plastoform avait sous-traité avec une grosse firme américaine pour une commande importante' (p.197).

4.3   325 000 francs *and Vailland*

The image which initially triggered Vailland's decision to write a work of fiction instead of pieces of journalism was the sight of one victim of the injection press: 'Je suis allé à Oyonnax et, dans un café, j'ai vu un manchot qui jouait aux cartes. On m'a dit qu'il jouait aux cartes toute la journée [...]. Le roman s'est organisé autour' (*27*, p.481).[8] This image of living death, of hopeless immobility, of a man prisoner of his body and his circumstances,

---

[8] In chapter 1 of Zola's novel *Travail* (1901), the 18-year-old Josine tells how a mutilating accident caused her to lose her job at a shoe factory: ' "une machine à piquer les bottines [...] m'a cassé un doigt. Il a fallu le couper"'; her right hand is bandaged up to the wrist. In a drunken rage Ragu, who has seduced and rejected her, throws her out of a bar. 'Dans la violence du geste, le pansement de la main droite venait d'être arraché, le linge rougit tout de suite d'une large tache de sang'.

corresponds closely to how Vailland saw himself each time his own life seemed to have come to a standstill. As well as being a spur to the composition of *325 000 francs*, Vailland's identification with the hapless victim of the injection press governs the way in which Busard is presented in the novel. At first, when Busard is 'en forme', this identification is given free expression: 'Quand Busard avait franchi la ligne blanche du col, j'avais vu dans son visage, dans le rejet de sa tête en arrière, qu'il éprouvait la même allégresse que lorsque je viens d'achever un chapitre dont je suis content' (p.33). This configuration of nobility, happiness and achievement reflects the positive associations that cycle racing held for Vailland. His identification with Busard is summed up in an isolated phrase which appears in the first two-page sketch for the novel: '— Moi, je veux vivre aujourd'hui' (Fonds RV). The phrase prefigures some of the slogans of May 1968, which Vailland would undoubtedly have welcomed, not only for its echoes, as a massive popular *fête*, of the Popular Front in 1936 and the Liberation in 1944, but above all as the expression of a yearning for a life lived with intensity. In the final version of *325 000 francs*, the phrase appears twice: during Busard's approach to Chatelard: '"Moi, dit-il violemment, je veux vivre aujourd'hui' (p.110), and after having a drink with Paul Morel: 'Je veux, dit farouchement Busard, vivre aujourd'hui!' (p.118). In the course of the novel, the narrator's attitude changes (see below, *4.6*): he cannot forgive Busard for losing (or misapplying) this *élan vital*. Vailland's own attitude to Busard's dispossession is, however, complex: on the political level, there is more at stake than a specific campaign against industrial accidents, or a general plea for working-class solidarity; on the personal level, Busard's failure holds up a mirror, and an uncomfortable warning, to his author. The issue is to find a stable and sustainable framework within which to set 'living for today' and 'living for tomorrow', transcending the opposition between the two. After a list of possible titles for his novel, Vailland adds: 'Quel gâchis — si aujourd'hui était plaisant, il n'y aurait pas de raison de se battre pour que demain soit différent' (Fonds RV). This suggests that the composition of *325 000 francs*, a novel directed towards external, public and political issues, brought Vailland face to face with long-standing inner conflicts (see above, chapter *1*). In punishing Busard for his inability to stand up to reality in the shape of Marie-Jeanne and the injection press, Vailland is also punishing himself.

In *325 000 francs*, the choice of characters' names often points to specific preoccupations on Vailland's part: his family, his personal mythology, or his attitude to a character. Busard has the widest range of associations: *un busard*: a buzzard; the character representing Vailland is named Milan (a kite) in *Les Mauvais Coups* and Duc (a horned owl) in *La Fête*; *une buse*: a fool; a failure (Belgicism: *il a été busé*); and also a pipe or conduit: at one point in the manuscript, Vailland even writes 'le busard éjecteur' in place of 'le conduit éjecteur' (p.152). The adjective *buté* emphasises Busard's stubborn-ness; when Busard comes to Jambe d'Argent's café, he is described as having 'l'air *buté*' (p.171), replacing 'sombre' in the manuscript. Finally, the suffix *–ard* is often derogatory in French; after a passage (p.163) on Busard's anxieties about time and death, he exclaims: 'Toquard' (p.164), replacing 'Idiot' in the manuscript; Vailland also changes the name of the union secretary from Signoret to Chatelard: the name in *–ard* associates him to some extent with Busard's failure.

With names as commonly used as 'Marie' or 'Jeanne', there is a risk of reading too much into their choice by an author; certainly Marie-Jeanne's double first name, as M. Picard points out (*37*, pp.336–37) combines petty-bourgeois connotations (Marie) and proletarian or communist echoes in Vailland's work (Jeanne): for example, Jeanne Gris is the name of the young communist lawyer who defends the imprisoned Rodrigue in *Bon pied bon œil*, becoming his lover and companion in political activism. It is also reminiscent of the *communard* poem, 'Les Mains de Jeanne-Marie' (R. Little, personal communication), by Rimbaud, the totemic poet of the adolescent Vailland, and of Eugène-Marie in *Un Jeune Homme seul*. The poem begins: 'Jeanne-Marie a des mains fortes, / Mains sombres que l'été tanna, / Mains pâles comme des mains mortes'. There is also, however, a bitterly ironic, even sarcastic, echo of the name Vailland used seven years earlier in a short piece for radio, 'Appel à Jenny Merveille' (*28*, p.151–76). Vailland's eventual choice of Lemercier for Marie-Jeanne's surname puts her firmly in the petty-bourgeois class. The name Morel, Vailland's mother's maiden name, suggests that, however paternally or fraternally Jules and his son Paul may feel and act towards Busard, they are not his true family. Vailland discovered in 1954 that Morel was the maiden name of Henri Bourbon's second wife (*34*, p.621). Although the narrator and Cordélia form a well-matched and united couple, she bears the name of King Lear's daughter ('What shall Cordelia do? Love, and be silent' — *King Lear*) making it possible to cast the narrator as Lear ('Come, let's away to prison [...] and hear poor rogues / Talk of court news; and we'll talk with them too, / Who loses, and who wins; who's in, who's out'). Certainly Vailland's Cordélia is an indispensable link ('corde-et-lia') between the narrator and the protagonists, especially Marie-Jeanne.

As with *Un Jeune Homme seul*, Vailland considered a number of titles for *325 000 francs*. Some were restrictive ('Des carosses [*sic*]-corbillards'); too specific ('Un poing c'est tout'); too revealing ('Départ impossible') or prosaic ('Busard et Marie-Jeanne', 'Aujourd'hui'). As a title, '325 000 francs' focuses on the means without revealing the ending, and reflects the major part played in the novel by financial calculations and considerations. At the end of the novel, it is suggested that an exact assessment of Marie-Jeanne's finances is the only basis for a sound judgment of her actions: '"Marie-Jeanne n'a jamais rien eu avec le vieux Morel, affirma fermement Cordélia. / — Faisons les comptes, dis-je, puisque c'est notre manière de vérifier l'intégrité de nos amis"' (p.240). For Vailland, money had long been associated with qualities which he valued (such as success with women), and lack of it had been a major source of frustration during his adolescence and thereafter until the success of *La Loi* in 1957. The process of making money is a significant theme in many of his novels and plays.

4.4   Thematic structure of 325 000 francs

The central unit in the thematic structure of *325 000 francs* consists of Busard, Marie-Jeanne and the injection press. On the plane of reality, this structure is not a complete triangle: the only link between Marie-Jeanne and the machine is Busard. On the symbolic plane, the configuration is different: on the one hand, there is the physically and morally enslaved Busard; on the other, there is the instrument of this enslavement, consisting of a mechanised Marie-Jeanne and an animated machine.

Busard

Busard can be contrasted with Eugène-Marie in *Un Jeune Homme seul*: Eugène-Marie is a hero in the making who finally asserts his potential: 'On peut apprendre beaucoup de choses en vingt-quatre heures' (*4*, p.194). Busard, however, is unable to use circumstances to his advantage, and loses heroic potential early in the novel. From chapter 1 to chapter 7, Busard gains in self-awareness, but by the time he realises the exact nature of his economic and personal situation (pp.159–65), he has long since lost any margin of manoeuvre: '— Il n'y a rien à faire' (p.160). His thoughts come in the form of slogans: 'Il faut quitter au plus vite cette ville puante' (p.162), echoing Eugène-Marie's recitations of Rimbaud with his father: 'Le mieux est de quitter bien vite ce continent pourri' (*4*, p.51). Torn between conflicting ideas, Busard is unable to sustain any constructive thought: 'Il repoussa violemment l'idée qu'il désirait la voiture encore plus intensément que la présence de Marie-Jeanne [...]. Il repoussa violemment l'idée que les heures dans le snack-bar seraient peut-être du temps mort, comme celui auprès de la presse' (p.164).

All this comes about through Busard's double enslavement: to Marie-Jeanne, and to the machine. By the end of the cycle race, Busard's enslavement to Marie-Jeanne is established: 'Busard tourna la tête vers Marie-Jeanne. "C'est pour vous", cria-t-il' (p.44). In their relationship it is she who calls the shots (pp.53–69). In his desperation to win Marie-Jeanne, Busard tells Chatelard that he and Marie-Jeanne have to get married soon because she is pregnant (p.110), an occurrence which is invested with unheroic significance in *Un Jeune Homme seul* (*4*, pp.107–08: see above, *3.5*). During the scene in Jambe d'Argent's bar, after Busard has been drinking steadily, he is described thus: 'Busard se tenait un peu raide sur sa chaise, comme les jeunes gens des vieilles familles, qui ont été élevés sévèrement' (p.177). Through this parody of bourgeois respectability, Busard is associated with Marie-Jeanne: 'Les passants la voient tout au long de l'année, assise bien droite sur une chaise de paille à haut dossier' (p.9).

As for the machine, he imagines that he can control it as well as he can ride his racing cycle: 'Busard s'était juré de respecter la règle de sécurité. Il ne touchera jamais au coupe-circuit' (p.104). Thus he underestimates the dangers for him of the work he has embarked on, just as he puts his failure to win the Circuit de Bionnas down to bad luck (p.57). Meanwhile Marie-Jeanne 'revoyait Busard et le Bressan échappés du peloton, analogues à des enfants qui lancent leurs billes sur un jeu de boules où des adultes sont en train de calculer leurs coups [...]. Cela ne pouvait que mal finir' (p.59). Marie-Jeanne's pessimism is only half justified: le Bressan wins the Circuit de Bionnas the following year as well (p.241), but Busard is doubly mistaken: in his estimation of his own abilities, and in his dependence on Marie-Jeanne.

Morally captive to Marie-Jeanne, Busard becomes physically captive to the press. There are several stages in the process of moral, physical and mental degradation. He realises that he is no longer obliged to refuse a drink (p.117); he is less desperate to sleep with Marie-Jeanne; when she finally relents, his own physical decline has already begun (p.151); he feels a sense of worthlessness, humiliation and helplessness (pp.159–60) which he desperately tries to shrug off (pp.163–64); he loses sleep, and the difference between sleep and wakefulness is gradually abolished for him (pp.148, 151, 154, 201, 215, 221); he loses a sense of perspective or proportion about what he is doing and why (pp.176, 191, 216–17). In the final scene at the factory, Busard's attention to a minor fault in the operation of the automatic press, the one which produces 'les gobelets du même bleu que les yeux de Marie-Jeanne' (p.225), distracts him from what is happening to 'his' machine. He has enough knowledge to be able to make it work again, but not enough to know what is wrong with it. The law of the race is inexorable: to win, one must take the shortest time of all the competitors. The law of the machine (the penalty for not keeping up the work-rate) has been internalised by Busard: ' "Si je replace le coupe-circuit, je perds plus d'une minute, j'ai l'amende et je n'aurai pas fini demain à huit heures." C'était absurde' (pp.226–27). He is now wholly in the grip of an inner necessity: 's'il avait conçu qu'il était possible de transgresser, il y a longtemps qu'il aurait déclaré forfait' (p.227).

Marie-Jeanne

Marie-Jeanne's place in the thematic structure of the novel is circumscribed by the need to avoid two extremes: demonise her, and Busard's responsibility for his own downfall is diminished; exonerate her, and Busard's mutilation could appear to be simply a matter of bad luck.

Marie-Jeanne's caution and pessimism arise from her class background, and from specific experiences at the hands of men (pp.66–69). This sequence plays a vital part in the construction of the reader's view of Marie-Jeanne. It shows that she has had sexual experience; but does this mean that Busard's accusation, in the final chapter (p.239), that she has slept with Jules Morel in order to obtain the 300 000 francs needed for Jambe d'Argent's bar, is justified? In the first version of the novel, Busard's suspicions are shown to be well founded, whereas the final version suggests that Busard is mistaken. Vailland notes, at the end of a plan for chapters 3–8: 'La trahison de M. J.' (Fonds RV). In the first version of the scene where Busard overhears Marie-Jeanne and Jules Morel, Morel's first words are 'Une seule fois encore et je te foutrai la paix', and three lines later she says to him: 'Il fallait réfléchir avant' (Fonds RV). In the final version, the words Busard overhears are: 'ensuite, je te foutrai la paix', and Marie-Jeanne says: 'Il fallait réfléchir' (p.238). The character of the subsequent scene (pp.240–42), where the narrator accuses Cordélia of lying to protect Marie-Jeanne, depends on whether the narrator's suspicions are justified. In the final version, Cordélia extracts the explanation from le Bressan, who has just won the Circuit de Bionnas for the second year (p.241): it was he who, secretly, had paid Jambe d'Argent the

300 000 francs (p.242). Both the narrator and Busard refuse to believe this, but the balance of probability is in Marie-Jeanne's favour. A hint of ambiguity is retained, however, when Jules Morel says to Busard: 'Je connais ta fiancée', then notices that the inside of the press needs wiping down: ' "La peau de chamois" ' (p.211). The reference to the chamois leather, added at a late stage of composition, suggests that Morel knows the inside of both the press and Marie-Jeanne, and is inviting Busard to look after both of them. In encouraging Busard's individualistic dream, Morel is acting as a 'faux père' ('Excellente idée, le snack-bar, c'est l'avenir. [...]. Tu vois que tout le monde peut devenir capitaliste', pp.210–11), in contrast to Chatelard's defensive, but nevertheless paternal and protective attitude.

Throughout the novel, Marie-Jeanne is presented as acutely aware of her vulnerability; her expectation of a relationship with a man is that she will be prey for a hunter or, in the narrator's formulation (pp.132–33), a slave to a master. Depending on the overall circumstances, however, the prey can become the hunter. This reversibility is underlined in a passage added at a late stage; the narrator suggests to Cordélia that Marie-Jeanne has the upper hand, but only for the time being: 'Elle a le jeu maître, parce qu'ils sont demandeurs. Le rapport se renverserait dans l'instant même où leur désir éveillerait un écho chez elle. Fondamentalement, ce sont eux qui sont les plus forts, parce qu'ils sont des hommes" ' (p.132). The second sentence here is incompatible with the original conception of a Marie-Jeanne who was capable of betraying Busard with Jules Morel: it is precisely her lack of warmth that makes her a powerful figure, both in the eyes of Busard and in her symbolic role as the instrument of Busard's downfall: the fatal impetus comes from Busard himself.

Marie-Jeanne's power over Busard is suggested in a series of violent images, arising from details of her physical appearance: her fingernails (p.9); her voice (p.48); her teeth (p.60); her sudden colouring (p.61); her eyes (p.139); the skin between her breasts (p.141); her clothes (p.142). As Recanati concludes: 'Marie-Jeanne est constamment liée au sang, à la mutilation et à la mort' (*36*, p.226). Chapters 2 and 4, describing Marie-Jeanne's appearance and how she relates to men, alternate with chapters 3 and 5, which show the operation of the press, and its effects on the operatives. In chapter 2, Marie-Jeanne eats one of the liqueur chocolates that Cordélia has brought her: 'Marie-Jeanne poussait le bonbon tout entier dans sa bouche, l'écrasait lentement, fermait les yeux, et le maintenait longtemps avec la langue contre le palais' (p.52). The image of Marie-Jeanne slowly crushing the chocolate in her mouth, and not between her teeth, is comparable to the description of the press in chapter 3: 'Ce ventre peut à l'occasion se transformer en mâchoire capable de broyer n'importe quel poing' (p.95). She is as smooth and polished on the outside as the inside of the injection press: 'Le ventre de la presse à injecter est délicat et précieux' (p.95); 'C'est tout le visage de Marie-Jeanne qui est toujours exactement poncé' (p.139). It is the 'female' part, not the 'male' part of the press which moves, just as Marie-Jeanne moves between saying yes and no: 'elle lui a donné de l'espoir, elle a dit non, elle a dit oui, elle s'est reprise; le voilà enchaîné' (p.142). Like the injection press, her power over Busard is all the greater for being concentrated in one small area.

The scene where Marie-Jeanne comes to see Busard at work (pp.217–21) comes towards the end of the six-month period, Marie-Jeanne's distrust of the factory and all it represents (p.68) having kept her away until then. At this point, the only time that Marie-Jeanne and the press are shown together, she is for once not at all machine-like: 'Elle revoyait les épaules de Busard inondées de sueur, elle était bien plus émue que quand elle l'avait eu nu contre elle' (pp.220–21). Busard is now completely in the power of the machine and of Marie-Jeanne; her protectiveness at this point seals his fate.

The machine

Busard's misconception is to believe that he is master of the machine, just as he is unaware of the extent to which he has allowed himself to be dominated by Marie-Jeanne.

The injection press is the embodiment of the power Marie-Jeanne exercises, through being a *forme vide* (see below), over Busard. Thematically, the machine is associated more with *matière* than with *forme*, but in effect it appears as a fusion of the two: empty form and meaningless substance, absurd but all-powerful. The name of the factory, Plastoform, combines both elements; the machine is androgynous: 'Le ventre est composé de deux parties, l'une mâle, l'autre femelle' (p.93); the product of this androgynous union is an absurd parody of a luxury object, either red coaches (Busard's dream-cars) or black hearses (real death) (p.96); the machine is highly dangerous, despite all attempts to tame it (pp.95, 102–03); although the workers joke about it (p.94), the machine imposes an atmosphere of respect: 'La lente cadence [...] donnait aux gestes des ouvriers une apparence de solennité. Ils ne parlaient, ne riaient, ni ne chantaient' (p.99); above all, the machine induces a hypnotic sleep-like state: 'le risque était que l'ouvrier s'endormît, la main dans le ventre de la presse' (pp.101–02).

The process of production is described as one of giving birth, with the operative as midwife: 'Busard retira du ventre de la presse [...] un objet' (p.97); he cuts 'le reste du cordon ombilical de matière plastique' (p.98). The process also resembles defecation, or a small child's fantasy about giving birth orally; but it carries at the same time a threat of castration, even of self-mutilation. As Picard puts it: 'Busard s'accouche de lui-même'; but by so doing 'il se châtre [...]; il s'accouche indéfiniment sans jamais sortir du ventre maternel' (*37*, pp.338–39). For Picard, the machine is a vast, self-sufficient Mother-figure. Recanati remarks on the frequency with which Vailland introduces machinery into his novels, for example the *trabucco* in *La Loi* or the bowling alley in *La Truite*: 'Chaque fois les machines sont inquiétantes: elles grincent, elles happent, elles mordent, elles emprisonnent, elles peuvent mutiler' (*36*, p.228).

There are numerous parallels and contrasts between the scene where Busard first encounters the press (pp.92–104) and the description of the hours and minutes leading up to the accident (pp.223–31). Busard starts work with the firm intention of not interfering with the safety mechanism, believing that he can cope with the additional strain: 'Il n'était pas lié à la presse pour la vie, comme la plupart de ses camarades d'atelier' (p.104). His illusion, throughout chapters 3–7, is that he can escape this fate by an exercise of will; however, as with Eugène-Marie in part 1 of *Un Jeune Homme seul*, willpower is not enough. In chapter 7, he ignores all the warning signs, believing to the last that 'la vivacité du geste et l'extrême attention qu'il exigeait, contribueraient à l'empêcher de s'endormir' (pp.228–29). Busard seeks life ('je veux vivre aujourd'hui!') but is unable to build a basis for a new life; instead, he is drawn down by Marie-Jeanne and the machine into non-life: work on the machine is the antithesis of life, 'une entreprise attentatoire au principe même de la vie' (p.207). In *Drôle de jeu*, Marat stresses the inherently humiliating nature of wage labour, and condemns both acceptance and the search for an individual way out: 'Manœuvre qui se résigne à rester manœuvre, c'est une *pauvre putain*. Ouvrier qui veut "s'en sortir", qui rampe, lèche ou ruse', he and his wife 'ce sont de *sales putains*. Mais qu'il devienne militant, tout est changé. L'usine, le bureau, le magasin n'est plus un bordel, c'est un champ de bataille' (*1*, p.287). In *325 000 francs*, this pessimistic analysis is echoed in Busard's cry: 'Putain de moi-même' (p.160), when he realises just what his price is as a wage labourer.

In the course of his work on the press, Busard gradually loses sight of his objective, which is to 'possess' Marie-Jeanne (pp.164, 191). The machine cannot be a means to possessing Marie-Jeanne, because Marie-Jeanne is the machine, and the machine is Marie-Jeanne. Whereas in *Un Jeune Homme seul* Eugène-Marie emerges from the dual mother-child relationship and achieves individual heroic stature in a worthy collective cause, in *325 000 francs* Busard declines from a state of ambition, *forme* and wakefulness to one of somnolence, mutilation, dependence and resentment. For Picard, 'La hargne de Busard manchot est celle d'un enfant puni et humilié, "repris en main" par sa mère, comme le prouvent son ivrognerie, son emménagement dans la Cité Morel et son projet de retourner travailler à la presse' (*37* p.345).

Integrated into the structure of *325 000 francs* are a number of pairs of thematic opposites which are contrasted but never resolved, giving the novel a particular density of meaning. Two of them are discussed below:

'Forme' and 'matière'

325 000 francs is composed of two parallel but contrasting cycles: the race (chapter 1) and the work on the press (chapters 3–7). The link, and the contrast, between the two cycles is expressed through the notions of *forme* and of *matière*. The cycle of *forme* (chapter 1) is followed by the cycle of *matière* (chapters 3–7). In chapter 1, the term *forme* encapsulates the narrator's sympathy and admiration for Busard: for both of them, *la forme* is an agreeable state of mind and body, and essential for their efforts to succeed, whether it is a matter of winning a race or writing a book. The cycle race is the one positive manifestation in the novel of Busard's desire to 'vivre aujourd'hui' (p.110): it offers a challenge to human endeavour, the possibility of exhilaration, the triumph of mind over matter, or at least of *forme* over matter: 'pour que l'athlète soit *en forme*, il faut [...] que la matière soit devenue forme' (p.32). Work on the press represents the very opposite; Busard realises the difference almost as soon as he has begun: 'Il ne faisait plus partie de la cohorte des héros [...]. Il n'aurait jamais plus rien à sacrifier à *la forme*. Il était rentré dans le rang' (p.117). For the writer, form is indissociable from content, from the finished product: 'Pour l'écrivain aussi, quand il a atteint la maturité et quand il a quelque chose à dire, la *forme* devient la préoccupation essentielle' (p.33).

The images of *forme* and *matière* are the basis of a further contrast, between *forme(s) pleine(s)*, associated with something living, substantial, and valid on its own terms, and *forme(s) vide(s)*, associated with inert, life-denying *matière*. This contrast is embodied in Juliette Doucet and Marie-Jeanne. The descriptions of Juliette (pp.13, 168–69) leave no doubt as to her 'formes pleines' (*39*, p.487), a stimulus to the imagination of her author and of the men of Bionnas, young and old. As *matière*, however, she is as ephemeral as victory in a race: her sex-appeal will not last (pp.170,

238). In Jambe d'Argent's bar, Busard sees Juliette and Marie-Jeanne as alternatives: 'Tu es bien plus belle que Marie-Jeanne. Tu es meilleure qu'elle. Je me sens mieux avec toi. Pourquoi est-ce que j'aime Marie-Jeanne?' (p.176), but Juliette does not take him seriously. The choice for Busard lies not between two young women, but between two ways of looking at life: there would be no point in Busard attaching himself to Juliette in the way that he has to Marie-Jeanne who in contrast to Juliette is, in Petr's words, 'une forme vide' (*39* p.487). As such, she cannot form part of a couple: in 1962 Vailland writes that the woman 'est la matière du couple, l'homme la forme, et dans les meilleurs cas la flamme; elle est la partie végétale animale de l'humain, où l'homme pensant, connaissant, retourne un moment pour retrouver matière et se faire flamber avec' (*28*, p.693). Far from being universal, Marie-Jeanne's sex-appeal is to 'les hommes d'âge mûr et les vieillards' (p.141). As for Busard, 'Il a choisi Marie-Jeanne, parce que de toutes les femmes qu'il connaît, elle est la plus précieuse' (p.142). She is a luxury item, an object, an empty shell. More specifically, the narrator suggests that, between Busard and Marie-Jeanne, there is no fusion such as occurs at the climax of a good cycle race, or indeed every forty seconds during the operation of the injection press (p.94). On the contrary, 'J'imaginai que le désir tenait peu de place dans sa prédilection; les héros ne sont pas nécessairement des voluptueux' (p.142).

'Eveil' and 'sommeil'

When Busard is *en forme* in chapter 1, the narrator declares: 'J'imaginais l'exaltation de Busard et je l'enviais' (p.28), but his pursuit of cycling success is shown to be a dream when, in chapter 2, he unfolds before Marie-Jeanne his vision of his future career (pp.57–58). The chapters that follow show him dreaming in the face of reality: the work on the press induces a state of torpor, the very opposite of being *en forme*. Busard soon realises this, and the thought which brings tears to his eyes is that he had become 'pareil aux vieux ouvriers qui n'ont plus d'espérance, et qui boivent à la sortie de l'usine, pour substituer la chaude somnolence de l'alcool à la morne somnolence du travail machinal […]; '*la forme* est au contraire l'extrême pointe de l'éveil' (pp.117–18). The two words *somnolence* and *éveil* sum up the balance-sheet of the transaction Busard has entered into, underlining the gap between what he thinks he can achieve (his dream), whether in the race or at the press, and the effect on him (reality) of his attempt to use the press as a means to win Marie-Jeanne. He acts heroically in a situation where heroism is futile.

4.5   325 000 francs: narrative structure

The narrative structure of *325 000 francs* is linear: there are no flashbacks such as those in part 2 of *Un Jeune Homme seul*. The narrative is organised in two sequences.

The first sequence (pp.15–45) presents the cycle race in terms of closed circles, rather than as a straight line: the first three words of the novel ('Le Circuit cycliste', p.5) emphasise, twice, the notion of a circle; the route of the race forms a figure 8 (p.14): a closed figure, a double circuit; infinity, endless repetition; the same route is covered three times (p.14). The second sequence (pp.91–231) is thematically and structurally parallel to the first. It covers a precisely defined period of time, just as the race follows a fixed route, and attention is focused on the same two men; the task consists of a series of endlessly repeated movements (p.113), like riding a racing cycle, but carried out on a static machine: there is no progression; the difficulties and dangers make both tasks an *épreuve*, but the second task is a parody of the first: each stage marked off on the calendar (pp.192, 209) becomes a link in a chain of absurdity. The final stages of both tasks are commented on by an audience: in the cycle race, the crowd's 'il saigne... il saigne...' (pp.39, 43); at the factory, comments from Jules Morel, Chatelard and a visitor from Paris, Hélène, and Marie-Jeanne. The two men approach the race, and the work on the press, and are affected by them, in opposing ways, and at the end of both cycles le Bressan is unscathed, while Busard is not.

In both tasks, Busard sees himself as moving forward (in space or time) on a linear course towards a goal; to the observer, however, his trajectory in both cases is circular, involving repetition and decline or degradation: a living death. The narrator compares Busard's state of mind in the early stages of his work at the press to that of a racing cyclist going all-out for a bonus, and adds the comment that 'Toutes les passions provoquent le même affolement, la même course éperdue dans un couloir sans issue' (p.117). The inevitability of the conclusion is shown at the beginning of the 'second cycle' of *325 000 francs*: it is the fate which awaits every worker at the presses (including Busard), condemned to work longer hours in order to buy more goods (p.68); a few pages later, a parallel path is laid out before le Bressan, and any other small farmer (pp.75–76). Both accounts, hammering home the inevitability by repeated use of the future tense, end with the words: 'et rien d'autre jusqu'à la mort'. Busard is doomed to remain in Bionnas, condemned either to intra-uterine life, or to death. The nightmare that threatens the individual in headlong flight along a linear path, is that of coming to a standstill, as the injured Busard does, 30 metres from the top of the last climb of the race (p.43) — unlike le Bressan, who recovers strongly from the *coup de pompe* (pp.35–37). In his work on the press, Busard is brought to a standstill by Marie-Jeanne's letter (pp.120–22) and by the threatened strike (pp.193–96). Le Bressan's reasons for agreeing to Busard's proposition are in keeping with the closely ordered circumstances of his present and future life (p.80–81): there is no need for him to daydream. Conversely, Busard has daydreams of the future, as a racing cyclist (p.57–58), the owner of a Cadillac (p.104) or of a chain of snack-bars (p.150). In *Un Jeune Homme seul*, Eugène-Marie daydreams behind his window of sexual success with a working girl; but Eugène-Marie, unlike Busard, is well aware of the unrealistic nature of his dream (*4*, pp.59–61).

This interplay of cyclical and linear trajectories, both leading nowhere, is underpinned by repeated use of the figure 8, which, Vailland had written in *Un Jeune Homme seul*, when rotated through 90 degrees, gives ∞, the 'zéro jumelé qui, en mathématiques, symbolise l'infini, suggère l'idée du triomphe total, parfait, qu'il est impossible de remettre en question' (*4* p.40). The dual symbol, 8/∞ (although the symbol for infinity is ∞, infinity is often thought of as a straight line continuing for ever), draws together space and time, cyclical and linear motion, enclosure and infinity:[9] 'Le Circuit de Bionnas est en forme de huit' (p.14); 'La presse fonctionne dans le sens horizontal' (p.92); Busard fails at both. A horsefly pesters the narrator and the others following the race: 'j'essayais vainement de l'écraser avec un journal plié en huit' (p.18); in the race, le Bressan wears a white jersey with the number 8, and wins; Busard's six months' work on the press begins at 8 a.m. and is due to end at 8 p.m., but he loses. Safe in the circle of his life, le Bressan is unaffected by the work at the press: 'ce qui ne demande pas d'effort n'est pas un travail', even when the work rate is doubled: 'Zéro plus zéro égale zéro' (p.198). There is no risk for le Bressan that the two zeros, side by side, will combine into the symbol for infinity.

In chapter 7, the Paris-Nice road is referred to for the first time as 'la Nationale 7' (p.210), the figure 7 corresponding to the straight line of Busard's dream, the open road; but in chapter 8 the town of Bionnas closes round Busard and Marie-Jeanne; le Bressan, carrying the number 8, wins the Circuit a second time.

4.6   325 000 francs: *narrative perspective*

Un Jeune Homme seul is narrated, like the three novels which preceded it, in traditional third-person style. For *325 000 francs*, Vailland turns to the device of a narrator which he had used for the first time in *Beau Masque*. Although in both cases the narrator can be identified as an *alter ego* of Vailland himself, there are

---

[9] Alain Robbe-Grillet's *Le Voyeur* (1955), a novel which in other respects contrasts sharply with *325 000 francs*, contains several references to '(en forme de) huit' and twice to a 'huit couché'. But these form part of a system of spatial and spatio-temporal signs and symbols: horizontals, diagonals and verticals; rectangles and triangles; parallel lines and 'trajectoires'. In both novels, arithmetical, chronometric and financial calculations figure prominently: derisory, disconnected from reality, they suggest repetitiveness and inevitability. Coincidentally, a bicycle plays a key role in the narrative structure of *Le Voyeur*, perhaps reflecting the interest in the Tour de France aroused by the three successive victories in 1953–55 of the Frenchman Louison Bobet, 'le grand Bobet'.

significant differences. The narrator of *Beau Masque* is involved in the lives of the characters. Like Vailland since 1951, he lends his support as a journalist to the workers' struggle, helping Pierrette Amable to draft a tract for the union (*5*, p.285). He is friendly with both bourgeois and working-class characters, but shares the views of Pierrette; his approving voice in the reader's ear ensures that he fulfils an ideological as well as a narrative function. In the first drafts of *325 000 francs*, the narrator is a communist journalist who is making a study of the development of the plastics industry: this reflects the origins of the novel (see above, *4.1*). In the final version, however, he is an intellectual who likes to be surrounded by 'l'animation des villes ouvrières, à l'heure de la sortie des ateliers' (pp.5–6), and who has already met Marie-Jeanne several times (p.7): an idealised version of Vailland himself, detached, serene, benevolent, interested in people, empathising with Busard (p.28). The serenity of the narrator is put to the test when Busard, in order to win Marie-Jeanne, abandons his cycling ambitions: 'Il me plaisait, tant qu'il voulait gagner le Tour de France. Maintenant qu'il fait des bassesses pour devenir boutiquier, il me dégoûte' (p.125). The narrator associates Busard's abdication in the face of Marie-Jeanne with the lack of combativity of the people of Bionnas. It is as if the masochism displayed by Busard in his subservience to Marie-Jeanne brings out a latent sadism in the narrator, who makes Busard the scapegoat for what is not, in socio-economic terms, his fault (pp.142–43).

Marie-Jeanne confides readily in Cordélia (pp.47–54, 126–29), and these 'confidences' are then relayed to the narrator (pp.65–67, 129–30). Cordélia's comments relativise the narrator's pronouncements on the action, making them simply the expression of one man's point of view. He abandons his earlier view of Marie-Jeanne ('Marie-Jeanne avait le naturel qui n'est plus l'apanage que du peuple', p.49) after she has turned Busard down: 'Si j'étais Busard, comme je préférerais la grosse Juliette à cette petite bourgeoise de Marie-Jeanne' (p.125), and launches into a philosophical demonstration of the ambiguities of the master-slave relationship. Cordélia's response is dismissive: 'Tu m'ennuies.

Comment allons-nous faire pour réconcilier Marie-Jeanne et Busard?' (p.135). When challenged by Marie-Jeanne to tell her what he thinks, he retreats to a position based on male solidarity: 'j'aime beaucoup Busard et je préférerais que vous ne le fassiez pas souffrir' (p.140). Cordélia's judgements, on the other hand, are presented as trustworthy, for example during the cycle race (p.35), or when she and the narrator are discussing Marie-Jeanne (pp.65–66).

In 1961, comparing *La Fête* and *La Loi* unfavourably with *325 000 francs*, in terms of narrative technique, Vailland claims that: 'En introduisant le narrateur comme tel, non comme témoin impartial, dieu arbitraire, mais comme enquêteur actif, modifiant nécessairement les situations, on garde les plans multiples de l'histoire' (*28*, p.654). Certainly the narrator and Cordélia are 'active investigators', but it is hard to conclude that they 'modify the situations' of Busard and Marie-Jeanne: their support is not enough to make him win the race (chapter 1), in the efforts to reconcile the young couple they are just two voices among many (chapter 4), and Cordélia is unable to convince Busard of Marie-Jeanne's good faith over the money (chapter 8). Indeed, by attempting to intervene in the lives of Busard and Marie-Jeanne, both the narrator and Cordélia become part of the absurdity of the situation the narrator so vehemently denounces: 'Toute cette affaire est absurde' (p.125). The discussions between them (pp.123–36), while interesting and even humorous, shed little light on what is at stake for Busard and Marie-Jeanne at this crucial point in their lives. Their interventions are prompted by admiration (pp.33, 125), compassion (p.140), or simple curiosity (pp.138–40), rather than by ideological considerations.

The narrator thus fulfils a subjective function, shown in his interactions with Cordélia and his personal views on Busard, Marie-Jeanne and Chatelard, and an objective function as an informed observer of the socio-economic realities faced by the workers in Bionnas. In this way the link is preserved between *325 000 francs* as a work of fiction and the real-life campaign against industrial accidents, and a unity of tone is maintained between the chapters in which the narrator and Cordélia appear, and chapters 3, 5 and 7, from which they are absent.

4.7 Interpretations of 325 000 francs

325 000 francs was given wide publicity in the PCF press, and was serialised in *l'Humanité* from 22 December 1955 to 3 February 1956. Extracts were read and discussed at CGT meetings, fulfilling to some extent the original purpose of Vailland's investigation. This publicity helped to establish *325 000 francs* among a wider readership. When the novel first appeared, critics on both right and left assumed that it carried a political message, and that this message was that 'on ne fait pas sa révolution tout seul'. Some critics on the right saw the novel as mere political propaganda. A majority, however, praised *325 000 francs* for its social and psychological observation and its literary qualities.

In 1963, Vailland made a number of claims for his novel: '*325 000 francs*, le meilleur de mes romans, vrai rêve, rêve vrai, une vraie histoire qui peut être interprétée totalement par Freud, par Marx, et encore bien d'autres, elle a toutes les faces possibles de la réalité' (*28*, p.712). This implies that *325 000 francs* can sustain a number of different readings. Is this claim justified? The accident which happens to Busard, although a product of the novelist's choice and control over his subject-matter, is plausible, even likely, in so far as Busard is representative and the circumstances are realistic. A local doctor interviewed in *l'Humanité-Dimanche* when *325 000 francs* was about to be serialised in *l'Humanité*,[10] and Vailland in *325 000 francs* (pp.103–04), both set out clearly the complexities and contradictions of the workers' practices (such as disconnecting the safety mechanism), the erratic behaviour of the presses and the causes and effects of fatigue. However, the doctor is quoted as implying that most accidents happen to 'outsiders', people who have never worked in a factory before, whereas in the novel it is le Bressan, the innocent outsider (pp.102, 198–99), who emerges

---

[10] S. Lachize, 'Aux sources du roman de Roger Vailland, *325 000 francs*', *l'Humanité-Dimanche* 18 December 1955.

unscathed, while Busard, who 'connaissait toute l'étendue de la tentation et du danger' (p.104) is maimed.

In *325 000 francs*, there seems to be no possibility of achieving political heroism through a collective struggle for a transformation of social conditions. This emerges unmistakably in the narrator's diatribe when everyone in Bionnas is trying to reconcile Busard and Marie-Jeanne; 'Tel est le ton de l'époque [...]. Le "courrier du cœur" a remplacé le code de l'honneur [...]. Cette société retombe en enfance' (p.137). In the manuscript, this phenomenon is traced back to earlier in the century: 'Cela commença après la première Guerre Mondiale, quand les écrivains [...] commencent à célébrer le culte de l'adolescent et à flétrir la condition abjecte de l'adulte. Après la Seconde Guerre Mondiale, c'est l'enfant qui est devenu sacré' (Fonds RV). Other passages in the manuscript confirm that Vailland saw this cult of youth and of childhood as springing from an awareness among adults that they had been unable to achieve a satisfactory model of adulthood. The narrator's outburst is followed by: 'C'est la règle à la veille des grandes révolutions' (p.137); however strong the evidence, Vailland refuses to accept it as the last word. This refusal remained constant with Vailland to the end of his life: in November 1964 he writes: 'Et nous voici de nouveau dans le désert. Mais je ne veux pas croire qu'il ne se passera plus jamais rien' (*28*, p.809).

This refusal is the key to the interpretation of *325 000 francs*: there is no heroic course of action or positive outcome consistent with the social and historical setting. The narrator expresses similar political views to the narrator of *Beau Masque*, who declares: 'cette société finit dans la démence' (*5*, p.87), and: 'Les temps merveilleux et terribles approchaient' (*5*, p.331). The difference is that in *Beau Masque* the narrator invests these political views in the story and in the heroine, Pierrette Amable, whereas in *325 000 francs* the narrator does not even look for, let alone hail the merits of, the 'bolcheviks' who will lead the revolution: the sense of an overall lack of combative fervour accumulates relentlessly. Apart from Chatelard's initial opposition, there is no hostility towards Busard at the factory: the strike after his accident is the result of a 'mouvement d'indignation' (p.244), not part of a concerted campaign. Any suggestion that the workers foresee anything beyond the next pay packet is absent from the final version of *325 000 francs*, whereas in the first version, where a dozen workers and union leaders are named, the possibility of the working class taking power is presented as a live issue, at least in the minds of these workers: 'Tous, sauf Rouzières et Chaillon, devenus sceptiques, sont persuadés que la classe ouvrière prendra le pouvoir, dans un temps plus ou moins bref, mais "qu'ils verront cela"' (Fonds RV). These sentiments echo Vailland's affirmation in *L'Humanité* a few months earlier: 'J'espère bien vivre assez longtemps pour voir le socialisme édifié en France' (*27*, p.394).

When, in *Beau Masque*, Pierrette challenges Vizille (a former communist Resistance leader) with the words: 'Tu veux faire la révolution tout seul?' (*5*, p.323), it is because he is trying to blow up a busload of CRS riot police; the phrase is a condemnation of individualist, anarchic actions that will harm the workers' cause. In *325 000 francs*, the phrase, when repeated by Chatelard (p.214), is a simple statement of economic realities. In the filmed version of *325 000 francs*, made for television in 1964, the part of the narrator is played by Vailland himself. At the end of the film, he draws a personal and a political conclusion from the story: 'on n'échappe pas à sa condition sans transformer la société qui vous a enfermé dans cette condition' (*37*, p.336). Thus, long after he had ceased to see himself as 'un écrivain au service du peuple' (*28*, p.753), Vailland emphasises the impossibility of 'faire sa révolution tout seul'. Both *Beau Masque* and *325 000 francs* can be seen as a denunciation of the growth of materialist aspirations, and increasing Americanisation, in the 1950s. In this perspective, Busard's mutilation represents the price to be paid by anyone who seeks to rise out of their class. When Hélène, seeing the state Busard is in, attempts to send him home to rest, the narrator condemns Busard's exploit, calling it: 'une entreprise attentatoire au principe même de la vie' (p.207).

Busard was likely to fail, but he was not destined to fail. If the novel had presented Busard as destined to fail, it would have been of little use to the PCF, either in the campaign against industrial accidents, or in the general cause of working-class solidarity. Even if Busard had succeeded in his aim, the freedom he would have gained is, in a capitalist society, illusory, merely another form of economic slavery.

Indeed, some critics have used the term 'tragedy' in connection with the novel, either in essence (Picard): 'c'est un chef-d'œuvre tragique, un livre que son unité même clôt sur soi' (*37*, p.334) or in part (Petr): *325 000 francs* n'est pas [...] une tragédie moderne, pour la raison essentielle que la *tragédie dans le roman* n'en est qu'un attribut' (*39*, p.513). If it was not necessary for Busard to be mutilated in order for the political demonstration to be effective, then the origins of the 'tragedy' lie elsewhere: in Vailland's inability to find, either within himself or around him, a means of enacting his ethic of heroism. The tragedy is Vailland's, not necessarily that of the people of Bionnas or elsewhere.

5. Vailland today: achievement and limitations

Like *Le Rouge et le noir* (1830) by Vailland's master, Stendhal, *Un Jeune Homme seul* is centred on the quest for self-fulfilment of a protagonist who, caught between conflicting values, is unable to anchor his personal philosophy in the real world. This conflict is the basis for several domestic and public scenes presented with conviction and intensity, and showing an acute psychological awareness. The change of perspective between part 1, where the reader is given privileged access to Eugène-Marie's thoughts, and part 2, where he is viewed from a distance, through his actions (or inaction), serves to make his transformation, towards the end of the novel, more dramatic, but perhaps less plausible in psychological terms. There is a similar contrast between part 1 and part 2 in terms of the detail with which period and milieu are portrayed: the detailed evocation of family life (in the Favart household and at the wedding) gives way to the presentation of much of the narrative within the framework of Marchand's enquiry, and more mythological and allegorical elements come to the fore. In the early chapters of part 1, the successive scenes of Eugène-Marie's family life create a vivid atmosphere which is dramatised by the imminence of the wedding, which is announced as early as chapter 2. Narrative unity is preserved: all the events of part 1 and much of part 2 lead up to the succession of scenes (Madru's funeral, the 'gifle', Jacques Madru's escape, Eugène-Marie's imprisonment) which form a fitting climax, drawing together all the elements presented or suggested hitherto. It is not surprising that, in the circumstances of mounting Cold War tension in which *Un Jeune Homme seul* was published in October 1951, critics on both right and left saw the novel as dominated by an overtly political message, and indeed, it is difficult not to see the novel as in some respects Vailland's calling-card addressed to the PCF (see above, chapter *1*).

325 000 francs, which has been in print continuously since its first publication in 1955, thanks largely to the Livre de Poche edition which first appeared in 1963, can be said to have achieved recognition as being of lasting merit and interest. This longevity is due in no small measure to the novel's unity of place, action and structure, and to the cohesion between the realistic portrayal of events and characters, and the psychological and political interpretations which arise from the action. The operation of the injection press, and of Busard at work, an inherently monotonous process, is invested with dramatically symbolic significance: all is not as it seems in this contest between a man engaged on a dehumanising task and a machine with ferocious animal and sexual power — an echo, on a reduced scale, of the miners and the voracious pit which swallows them up every day, in Zola's *Germinal*. The novel starkly documents a society on the verge of being transformed — not politically, but materially and aspiration-ally. Nevertheless, the novel leaves some important questions unanswered. Why is it a worthy ambition to want to be a professional racing cyclist, but not to want to run one or more snack-bars? In both cases, Busard is walking (or riding) away from the problems of his fellow-workers. What is wrong if the people of Bionnas want Busard to win Marie-Jeanne and the chance to escape, just as the crowd had wanted Lenoir, their local champion, to win the Circuit de Bionnas (*6*, p.45)? Behind the narrator's consistent expression of scorn and scepticism towards the modest aspirations of the people of Bionnas, one senses a fundamental ambivalence in Vailland's attitude: he understands why these ambitions are essentially material in nature, but he yearns to be associated with a more heroic struggle, one that will involve him at a deeper level. In 1958, Vailland acknowledged that: 'je n'ai pas encore résolu le problème clairement posé dans *Drôle de jeu* (et *325 000 francs*): pour l'ouvrier énergique et intelligent, sortir (s'affranchir) seul de sa condition ou s'affirmer ouvrier et homme de qualité en luttant révolutionnairement' (*28*, p.549). Chatelard's solution: 'changer le régime' (*6*, p.161) is rejected by Busard. The two points of view, individualist and collectivist, are contrasted, but not analysed, still less synthesised: there is no discussion of how the regime might be changed, or of the difficulties, under a collectivist system, of accumulating sufficient capital to ensure that all machines are automated, so that their operatives are released from the drudgery and dangers of manual labour.

The achievement of *Un Jeune Homme seul* and *325 000 francs* as novels is not, however, confined to their success as re-creations of closely observed social realities. In *Un Jeune Homme seul*, Vailland reaches beyond the specific circumstances of class and history which affected adolescents in 1920s France, to capture the processes — challenges, initiations — of growing up which all humans have to pass through in order to achieve maturity. In *325 000 francs*, there is an acute awareness of the interplay between socio-economic pressures and individual psychological motivations, and of the difficulties for men and women of making authentic and life-affirming choices. Writing in *Les Nouvelles littéraires* (20 May 1965), François Nourissier hails *325 000 francs* as 'un récit magnifique [...], qu'on relira dans cinquante ans quand on voudra comprendre ce que fut, vers 1955, l'embourgeoisement du prolétariat français'. In both novels, Vailland's handling of set-pieces shows considerable skill in the choice and ordering of material, and the orchestration of different voices. This is readily apparent in *Un Jeune Homme seul* at several points during the wedding, and at the funeral of Madru; in *325 000 francs*, examples include the closing stage of the cycle race and the whole of chapter 6, set in Jambe d'Argent's bar. These and other set-pieces are closely woven into the thematic, narrative, psychological and mythological texture of the novels as a whole. As in the novels of Stendhal, the reader is sufficiently familiar, when each sequence begins, with the setting, the characters and what is at stake, to enable the scene to unfold at a natural pace, and for unexpected events to emerge with all the drama of real-life surprises. The dramatic potential of successive scenes in each novel is enhanced by the directness and fluidity of Vailland's style. The result in both novels, but particularly in *325 000 francs*, is a density and economy of composition, in which each part contributes to the whole. It is for such qualities that *Un Jeune Homme seul* and *325 000 francs* can be said to support Picard's judgment on Vailland's work as a whole: 'Il est probable que son œuvre apparaîtra un jour comme l'une des plus importantes et des plus représentatives de la littérature française entre 1945 et 1965' (*37*, p.534).

Vailland's lasting achievement as a novelist lies in the acuteness of his observation of the world around him (and of himself as observer), and in his penetrating analysis of the nature of the social changes taking place in the 1950s, in particular the growth of aspiration towards material well-being among the working and lower-middle classes. His main limitation, as an observer and analyst of underlying social realities and trends, arises from his personally and ideologically inspired attempt to identify the course of an individual life with the march of History. At the end of *Un Jeune Homme seul*, the declarations of faith (by his wife and grandmother) in Eugène-Marie's future prowess and happiness (*4*, pp.182, 200), and, in *Beau Masque* and *325 000 francs*, the narrator's assertion of the imminence of revolution, appear to the reader less as a necessary outcome of the personal or social circumstances presented in each novel, or as the next stage in the onward march of History, than as the simple consequence of the turn of the wheel, bringing alternately good and bad fortune. For Picard, however, it is precisely 'l'extrême singularité de l'écrivain', who was constantly aware of the tragic dimension of human existence, which enabled Vailland 'de *formuler* tous les problèmes des hommes de notre temps, ceux que posent la condition virile, la réinvention du couple, la compréhension de la société, l'action politique' (*37*, p.534).

6. Fiction and social reality since 1960

Although the Cold War had brought about, particularly between 1947 and 1962, an intensification of ideological differences, centred in the USA and the USSR respectively — one reflected with acuity in literary theory and practice in France (see above, chapter 2) — this polarisation of attitudes soon began to recede. Already after 1950, as Vailland shows clearly in *325 000 francs*, French people's preoccupations were increasingly with improving their material well-being. The conflict between class-based political commitment to the PCF and individual family and home-based aspirations is reflected in the contrast between the Party's revolutionary rhetoric and its pragmatic policies in factories and town halls.

Since 1960, novels which 'formulate' the personal, social and political issues identified by Picard in 1972 have been characterised by diversity of subject-matter, ideological perspective, and stylistic treatment. For example, Bernard Clavel's powerful autobiographical series of four novels, *La Grande Patience* (1962–68), is set in the period 1937–1945, whereas Christiane Rochefort's *Les Petits Enfants du siècle* (1961) offers an irreverent, ideologically unfocused view of life in the faceless slab-like suburbs that had begun to spring up around most towns in France, prefiguring social attitudes, and their reflection in literature, more characteristic of later decades. Following the social and cultural upheaval of May 1968, Robert Linhart's *L'Etabli* (1978) tells the story of a young intellectual turned factory worker, in the footsteps of the posthumously-published *La Condition ouvrière* (1951) by Simone Weil, who had worked for a year (1934–35) in the Renault car factory. In their different ways and times, both Linhart and Weil enact the yearning identification of the young Eugène-Marie in *Un Jeune Homme seul* with the working class. All three bear witness to a personal ideology which idealised, not working men and women as individuals, but the shared condition of earning a living through manual labour — a condition which Vailland himself repeatedly characterised as slavery. Pascal Lainé's *La Dentellière* (1974) reverts to the portrayal from the outside, by a bourgeois novelist, of working-class characters: the author's interest in his characters is psychological and sociological, but not political or ideological. More prescient, perhaps, of future economic realities, is René-Victor Pilhes's *L'Imprécateur* (1974), with its elaborate satire on monolithic corporations, though without suggesting an appropriate response in the form of a political strategy or ideological stance: the satire appears to rest on the premise that the 'monolith' will collapse in ridicule, under its own portentous weight.

None of these, or other works of French fiction which address social, economic and political realities and issues, has had an impact in any way comparable, in their time, to that of Zola's *Germinal* or Barbusse's *Le Feu*. Realism in fiction is, ultimately, circumscribed by the constraints set by its subject matter: even the Resistance epic, which continued for decades to inspire numerous fictional and fictionalised accounts, such as Lucie Aubrac's *Ils partiront dans l'ivresse* (1984), could not compare with the sheer horror and devastation of the trenches of the first World War. The 'search for heroism' embodied in the very structure of *Un Jeune Homme seul* led Vailland to set his novel in the past; despite the contemporary setting of his next novel, *Beau Masque*, the would-be working-class heroes are as out of step with 'ces mornes années 1950...' (*5*, p.331) as the decadent heirs to an industrial fortune, also shown in the novel. Seen in this light, *325 000 francs* emerges, not only as an implacable and convincing portrayal of the impossibility of heroism in the banality of French society of the 1950s, but also as a reminder, fifty years on, of how little and how slowly the human condition changes, despite the multiplication of gadgetry.

In the space of a few decades, many of the conditions and processes described in *325 000 francs* have passed into history, or at least, the history of France. Over large areas of the globe, however, extractive and productive industry is carried out in conditions which, in Europe, North America and parts of Asia, are regarded as belonging to a past era. With the inexorable and sometimes catastrophic decline of heavy extractive and productive industry in Western Europe throughout the 1980s and 1990s, the monolithic 'working class' was no longer a statistical reality, further lessening its already much-reduced political and ideological strength and cohesion. The 'oppressed class' had become more fragmented than at any time in the previous 100 years: it was now made up of certain categories of lower-paid workers, and many of the unemployed. In the majority of the industrial conurbations, a growing and significant minority were first- and second-generation migrants; as well as the stresses and strains of life in France, the two generations' widely differing attitudes and lifestyles brought new tensions and clashes. These are well brought out in Azouz Begag's *Les Chiens aussi* (1995). Unlike Claire Etcherelli's *Elise ou la vraie vie* (1967), a sincere and moving evocation of love between a French woman and a North African, but written from a European's standpoint, in *Les Chiens aussi* it is the voice of the 'new underclass' itself which we hear, through the caustic, unsentimental but idealist first-person narrator, César. Now the respective roles of the two generations are reversed, compared to Busard's ideology-free stance in *325 000 francs*, which clashes with the socialist and communist ideals of his father and of Chatelard, respectively: in *Les Chiens aussi*, it is the young César who seeks a political and social if not ideological ideal, conflicting with his father's permanent concern to maintain the modest material dignity he has achieved, by keeping his head down and turning his back on political involvement. Neither César nor the narrator of *325 000 francs* can resign themselves to a society lacking the will to unite in the struggle for a political ideal.

Select bibliography

Works by Vailland

The Vailland archive is kept at the Médiathèque Elisabeth et Roger Vailland, 1, rue du Moulin-de-Brou, 01000 Bourg en Bresse. References in the text to this archive are noted 'Fonds RV'. Several hitherto unpublished pieces by Vailland have appeared since 1994 in the twice-yearly *Cahiers Roger-Vailland*, Bourg en Bresse, Les Amis de Roger Vailland.

For a comprehensive bibliography of published books and articles by Vailland, see *Cahiers Roger-Vailland* No 8, December 1997.

For a twelve-volume edition of novels, plays, travel writing, and selected articles by Vailland, edited by J. Recanati, see *Œuvres Complètes*, Lausanne, Editions Rencontre, 1967.

Unless otherwise stated, place of publication is Paris.

Novels

Page references to Vailland's novels are to the last edition listed below.

1. *Drôle de jeu*, Corrêa, 1945 (Prix Interallié); Buchet/Chastel 1957; Livre de Poche, 1972.
2. *Les Mauvais Coups*, Sagittaire, 1948; Grasset, Cahiers Rouges, 1991; Livre de Poche, 1972.
3. *Bon pied bon œil*, Corrêa, 1950; Grasset, Cahiers Rouges, 1994; Livre de Poche, 1973.
4. *Un Jeune Homme seul*, Corrêa, 1951; Livre de Poche, 1970; Buchet/Chastel, 1977; London, Methuen, ed. J. Flower and C. Niven, 1985; Grasset, Cahiers Rouges, 1992.
5. *Beau Masque*, Gallimard, 1954; Folio, 1972; Gallimard, L'Imaginaire, 1991; Livre de Poche, 1970.
6. *325 000 francs*, Corrêa, 1955; London, English Universities Press, ed. D. Nott, 1975; Buchet/Chastel, 1977; London, Routledge, ed. D. Nott, 1989; Livre de Poche, 1963 (this edition contains some typographical errors; on p 167, chapter VI is wrongly headed VII, and on p 181, chapter VII is wrongly headed VIII).

7. *La Loi*, Gallimard, 1957 (Prix Goncourt); Folio, 1972; Livre de Poche, 1970.
8. *La Fête*, Gallimard, 1960; Folio, 1973.
9. *La Truite*, Gallimard, 1964; Folio, 1974.

Plays

10. *Héloïse et Abélard*, Corrêa, 1947 (Prix Ibsen).
11. *Le Colonel Foster plaidera coupable*, Editeurs Français Réunis, 1951; Grasset 1973.
12. *Monsieur Jean*, Gallimard, 1959.

Other fiction

13. *Les Hommes nus* (1925), ed. C. Petr, Monaco, Editions du Rocher, 1996.
14. *La Visirova ou des Folies-Bergère jusqu'au trône* (*roman-reportage*, *Paris-Soir*, July–August 1933), ed. R. Ballet, Messidor, 1986.
15. *Un Homme du peuple sous la Révolution* (1938) (with R. Manevy), Corrêa, 1947; Gallimard, 1979.
16. *Cortès, le conquérant de l'Eldorado* (*roman-feuilleton, Paris-Soir*, November–December 1941), ed. J. Sénégas, Messidor 1992. Many scenes and themes in *Un Jeune Homme* seul and *325 000 francs* are prefigured here: comments by a crowd on the hero; the individual threatened by the inexorable advance of the pack; the vulnerable, tender individual beneath a tough, virile shell; linear time, without alternation (day – night, seasons), leading inexorably to death.
17. *Les Liaisons dangereuses 1960*, script for the film directed by R. Vadim, Julliard 1960.

Essays

18. *Marat-Marat: discours sur la méthode de la souveraineté* (1942), ed. R. Ballet and C. Petr, Le Temps des Cerises, 1995.
19. *Le Surréalisme contre la révolution*, Editions Sociales, 1948; Bruxelles, Editions Complexe, 1988.
20. *Le Saint Empire* (1950), ed. R. Ballet, Editions de la différence, 1978.
21. *Laclos*, Seuil, Ecrivains de toujours, 1953
22. *Expérience du drame*, Corrêa, 1953; Monaco, Editions du Rocher, 2002.
23. *Les Pages immortelles de Suétone: les Douze Césars*, Corrêa/Buchet-Chastel, 1962; Monaco, Editions du Rocher, 2002.

24. *Le Regard froid: réflexions, esquisses, libelles 1945–1962*, Grasset, 1963.

Journalism, travel

25. *Boroboudour* (1951), *Choses vues en Egypte* (1952), *La Réunion* (1964), Gallimard 1981.
26. *Chronique des années folles à la Libération 1928/1945* (recueil d'articles), ed. R. Ballet, Editions Sociales, 1984; Buchet/Chastel, 2003. Other press articles from this period have been reprinted in issues of the *Cahiers Roger-Vailland*.
27. *Chronique d'Hiroshima à Goldfinger 1945/1965* (recueil d'articles), ed. R. Ballet, Editions Sociales, 1984.

Correspondence, journal

28. *Ecrits intimes*, ed. J. Recanati, Gallimard, 1968.
29. *Lettres à sa famille*, ed. M. Chaleil, Gallimard, 1972.
30. *N'aimer que ce qui n'a pas de prix* (1925–1965), ed. R. Ballet and C. Petr, Monaco, Editions du Rocher, 1995.

Works on Vailland

Biographical studies

The most comprehensive biography to date of Vailland is by Y. Courrière: (*34*). Short chronologies or biographical notes can be found in *31*, pp.275–281, *36*, pp.343–353, *37*, pp.13–20, *38*, pp.19–32, also in *6* (Routledge edition, 1989) pp.1–7, and the introductions to each section of *28* and *29*.

31. Chaleil, M., (ed.) *Entretiens 29: Roger Vailland*, Rodez, Editions Subervie, 1970.
32. Vailland, E. and R. Ballet (eds), *Roger Vailland*, Seghers, Ecrivains d'hier et d'aujourd'hui, 1973.
33. Vailland, E. (with P. Garbit), *Drôle de vie*, Lattès, 1984.
34. Courrière, Y., *Roger Vailland ou un libertin au regard froid*, Plon, 1991. A detailed biography, drawing extensively on interviews with people who knew Vailland, and on material in the Vailland archive in Bourg en Bresse. There are some errors of dates concerning Vailland's journalism, and on pp.636–37 the date of completion of *325 000 francs* is incorrectly given as May 1955.
35. Petr, C., *Roger Vailland, éloge de la singularité*, Monaco, Editions du Rocher, 1995.

Critical studies

36. Recanati, J., *Esquisse pour la psychanalyse d'un libertin: Roger Vailland*, Buchet/Chastel, 1971.
37. Picard, M., *Libertinage et tragique dans l'œuvre de Roger Vailland*, Hachette, 1972. A masterly thematic survey, providing extensive critical evidence for the essential unity of Vailland's preoccupations and the themes in his works.
38. Flower, J., *Roger Vailland, the man and his masks*, London, Hodder & Stoughton, 1975. The only monograph on Vailland in English; a study of Vailland and his works.
39. Petr, C., *Le Devenir écrivain de Roger Vailland (1944–1955)*, Aux Amateurs de Livres, 1988. A study of Vailland's development as a writer, centred on the first six novels; includes a detailed examination of the manuscript of *325 000 francs*; the dates of composition of *325 000 francs* are shown in the document reproduced on p.470.
40. *Europe: revue mensuelle* No 712–13, August–September 1988. Several articles on Vailland, including C. Petr, 'Roger Vailland dans le réalisme socialiste', pp.96–102.

Further reading

41. Caute, D., *Communism and the French intellectuals*, London, André Deutsch, 1964.
42. Gilbert-Lecomte, R., *Correspondance*, ed. P. Minet, Gallimard, 1971.
43. Flower, J., *Literature and the left in France: society, politics and the novel since the late nineteenth century*, London, Methuen, 1983.
44. Sirinelli, J.-F., *Génération intellectuelle: khâgneux et normaliens dans l'entre-deux-guerres*, Fayard, 1988.
45. Zeldin, T., *A History of French passions*, vol 1, Oxford, Clarendon Press, new edition, 1993: see chapter 10, 'Workers', pp.198–282.
46. Tame, P., *The Ideological hero in the novels of Robert Brasillach, Roger Vailland & André Malraux*, New York, Peter Lang, 1998: see Part III, 'Roger Vailland's "Bolshevik"', pp.179–305.
47. Sapiro, G., *La Guerre des écrivains, 1940–1953*, Fayard, 1999.